INVESTMENT SECURITIES PROGRAM GUIDE

USING THE HP-12C

D1609793

INVESTMENT SECURITIES PROGRAM GUIDE

USING THE HP-12C

W. SCOTT BAUMAN

JAROSLAW KOMARYNSKY

JOHN C. SISKA GOYTRE

McGRAW-HILL BOOK COMPANY

New York   St. Louis   San Francisco   Auckland
Bogotá   Hamburg   Johannesburg   London   Madrid
Mexico   Montreal   New Delhi   Panama   Paris
São Paulo   Singapore   Sydney   Tokyo   Toronto

1234567890   DOC/DOC   8932109876

Library of Congress Cataloging-in-Publication Data

Bauman, W. Scott, 1930–
Investment securities program guide using the
HP-12C.

Bibliography: p.
Includes index.
1. Investments—Data processing.   2. Business
mathematics.   3. HP-12C (Calculator) I. Komarynsky,
Jaroslaw.   II. Siska Goytre, John C.   III. Title.
HG4515.5.B38 1986   332.6′028   86–10599

ISBN 0-07-004104-0

The editors for this book were Martha Jewett and Georgia
Kornbluth, the designer was Elliot Epstein, and the production
supervisor was Thomas G. Kowalczyk. It was set in Electra by
ComCom.

Printed and bound by R. R. Donnelley & Sons Company.

CONTENTS

PREFACE

The past few decades have witnessed important developments in the fields of investment portfolio management and securities research analysis. These advances have helped investors make better decisions. However, these new developments also require investors to quantify financial information in a form that will be useful to them.

The Hewlett-Packard HP-12C pocket calculator has become very popular among individual and professional investors and business students because it is an advanced programmable calculator, uniquely designed to solve investment and portfolio problems easily and quickly. What are the reasons? The HP-12C can store up to 99 program lines, it has several basic programs already stored in its memory, and it uses reverse polish logic and a storage system which requires fewer keystrokes. Consequently, investment and portfolio problems that require many calculations can now be performed with special programs on the HP-12C conveniently and quickly. In fact, this calculator is so convenient that many analysts who use computers prefer to solve many investment problems on the HP-12C.

Therefore, we have developed specific programs on the HP-12C that are designed to solve many of the common problems faced every day by individual and professional investors. A casual review of the table of contents reveals the wide range of problems and investment decisions that this guide deals with. It covers the traditional tasks, such as measuring past rates of return and risk, and estimating present values, future rates of return, and yields to maturity; and it covers the newer tasks, such as measuring beta, bond duration, risk-adjusted returns, and bond swaps.

The organization and writing style of this guide enable both investment analysts and students of investments to use the HP-12C to analyze investment and portfolio problems. In each chapter we describe the computational tasks to be performed, present programs that are easy to use, and illustrate how to use them through clear examples.

The major topics in the guide are discussed in six chapters. Programs dealing with common stock investment decisions are presented in Chapter 1, those dealing with straight bonds are in Chapter 2, preferred stocks in Chapter 3, warrants and convertible securities in Chapter 4, stock options in Chapter 5, and portfolio management in Chapter 6. Chapter 7 deals with other problems in investment analysis. Reading references and an appendix of commonly used formulas appear after the last chapter.

Chapter
ONE

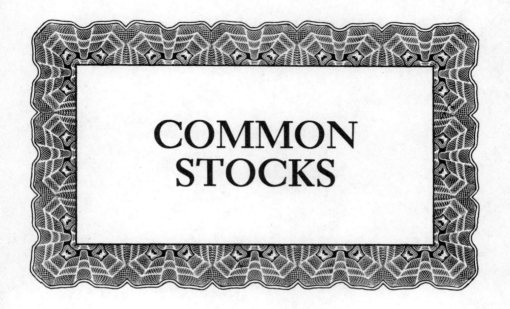

COMMON
STOCKS

Section
1-1
RETURN
MEASUREMENTS

SINGLE-PERIOD RATE OF RETURN

The *single-period rate of return* measures the rate of return a stockholder has obtained or expects to obtain by holding a stock investment during one period.

This return is calculated by dividing the total return—i.e., capital appreciation and dividends—by the beginning investment. (See the formula in the Appendix.)

The single-period rate of return may be calculated as follows:

1. Key in the ending price and press $\boxed{\text{ENTER}}$.
2. Key in the beginning price and press $\boxed{\text{STO 1}}$ $\boxed{-}$.
3. Key in the dividend and press $\boxed{+}$ $\boxed{\text{RCL 1}}$ $\boxed{\div}$.

Example: You bought a stock 1 year ago for $38 and subsequently received $2 in dividends. What is your rate of return if the stock sells now for $46?

Keystrokes	Display	Comment
46 $\boxed{\text{ENTER}}$	46.00	Enters ending price.
38 $\boxed{\text{STO 1}}$ $\boxed{-}$	8.00	Capital appreciation.
2 $\boxed{+}$ $\boxed{\text{RCL 1}}$ $\boxed{\div}$	0.26	Your return per dollar invested.

You thus obtained a return of 26 percent on your investment. Congratulations!

MULTIPERIOD RATES OF RETURN

Once a single-period rate of return has been calculated for a series of periods, a *multiperiod rate of return* can be calculated to determine the average rate of return earned on the investment over the entire time period. Discussed below are the arithmetic mean rate of return and the geometric mean rate of return.

Arithmetic Mean Rate of Return

The *arithmetic mean rate of return* is simply the arithmetic average of the single period rates of return. (See the formula in the Appendix.)

The following keystroke procedure may be used to calculate the arithmetic mean rate of return.

1. Key in a single-period rate of return.
2. Press $\boxed{\Sigma+}$.
3. Repeat steps 1 and 2 for all single-period rates of return.
4. Press $\boxed{g}$ $\boxed{\bar{x}}$.

Example: Suppose the single-period rates of return you obtained on your investment are as follows:

YEAR	RATE OF RETURN
1981	.21
1982	.17
1983	−.04
1984	.08
1985	.19

Keystrokes	Display	Comment
f CLEAR Σ	0.00	Clears statistics registers.
.21 Σ+	1.00	Enters rate of return in 1981.
.17 Σ+	2.00	Enters rate of return in 1982.
.04 CHS Σ+	3.00	Enters rate of return in 1983.
.08 Σ+	4.00	Enters rate of return in 1984.
.19 Σ+	5.00	Enters rate of return in 1985.
g x̄	0.12	Five-year arithmetic mean rate of return.
f 4	0.1220	

During the past 5 years you obtained, on the average, a return of 12.20 percent.

The arithmetic mean rate of return produces reasonable estimates in most instances. However, whenever there are either large changes in the rates of return or negative returns, as in the previous example, the arithmetic mean rate of return can significantly overstate or understate the true mean rate of return.

To overcome this problem, the geometric mean rate of return can be used instead of the arithmetic one.

Geometric Mean Rate of Return

The *geometric mean rate of return* is a compounded rate of return and thus avoids the generally optimistic bias introduced by the use of the arithmetic mean. (See the formula in the Appendix.)

The geometric mean rate of return can be determined by using the following procedure.

1. Key in a one-period rate of return and press ENTER .
2. Key in 1 and press + .
3. Repeat steps 1 and 2 and press x for the remaining observations.
4. Key in the number of one-period rates of return entered, and press 1/x y^x .
5. Key in 1 and press − .

Example: Using the single-period rates of return given in the previous example, calculate the geometric mean return.

Keystrokes	Display	Comment
.21 ENTER	0.21	Enters rate of return in 1981.
1 +	1.21	
.17 ENTER	0.17	Enters rate of return in 1982.
1 + x	1.42	
.04 CHS ENTER	−0.04	Enters rate of return in 1983.
1 + x	1.36	
.08 ENTER	0.08	Enters rate of return in 1984.
1 + x	1.47	
.19 ENTER	0.19	Enters rate of return in 1985.
1 + x	1.75	
5 1/x y^x	1.12	
1 −	0.12	Five-year geometric mean rate of return.
f 4	0.1180	

The 5-year geometric mean rate of return is 11.80 percent. The following program can be used to calculate the geometric mean return.

KEYSTROKES	DISPLAY	KEYSTROKES	DISPLAY
f P/R		1/x	06- 22
f CLEAR PRGM	00-	y^x	07- 21
x	01- 20	1	08- 1
STO 1	02- 44 1	−	09- 30
g GTO 00	03- 43,33 00	g GTO 00	10- 43,33 00
RCL 1	04- 45 1	f P/R	
RCL 2	05- 45 2		

REGISTERS			
n: Unused	i: Unused	PV: Unused	PMT: Unused
FV: Unused	R_0: Unused	R_1: Used	R_2: n
R_3–R_8: Unused			

The calculations may be made as follows:

1. Key in the program and press f CLEAR REG.
2. Key in the number of observations and press STO 2.
3. Key in 1 plus a single-year rate of return and press ENTER.
4. Key in 1 plus a second single-year rate of return and press R/S.
5. Repeat step 4 for all input values.
6. Press g GTO 04 R/S to find the geometric mean rate of return.
7. For a new case, return to step 2.

Example: Using the data from the previous example, determine the geometric mean rate of return.

Keystrokes	Display	Comment
5 [STO] 2	5.00	Number of observations.
1.21 [ENTER]	1.21	
1.17 [R/S]	1.42	
.96 [R/S]	1.36	
1.08 [R/S]	1.47	
1.19 [R/S]	1.75	
[g] [GTO] 04 [R/S]	0.12	Five-year geometric mean rate of return.
[f] 4	0.1180	

Section
1-2
RISK MEASUREMENTS

In addition to the rate of return, the risk inherent in an investment needs to be considered.

Risk can be determined by measuring an investor's uncertainty about the return outcome of an investment. The more uncertain the return outcome is, the higher the risk for the investment.

An investment's uncertainty is usually quantified by measuring the dispersion of returns around an expected mean value. The standard deviation is quite frequently used as a measurement of dispersion.

STANDARD DEVIATION

The *standard deviation* is a measure of the total investment risk assumed by the investor. The higher the standard deviation is, the higher the dispersion of the single-period returns around the mean, and, thus, the greater the total risk.

The HP-12C contains a program that permits calculation of the standard deviation (HP-12C "Owner's Handbook and Problem-Solving Guide," page 90).

Note that it is the "true-population" standard deviation and not the "best-estimate" standard deviation that we need to use. (See the formula in the Appendix.)

Example: What is the standard deviation of the annual rates of return obtained during the period 1981–1985?*

Keystrokes	Display	Comment
f CLEAR Σ	0.00	Clears statistics registers.
.21 Σ+	1.00	
.17 Σ+	2.00	
.04 CHS Σ+	3.00	
.08 Σ+	4.00	
.19 Σ+	5.00	
g x̄	0.12	Arithmetic mean annual rate of return.
f 4	0.1220	
Σ+	6.0000	
g s	0.0924	Standard deviation.

COEFFICIENT OF VARIATION

Another statistic of importance is the *coefficient of variation,* which is the ratio of the standard deviation to the expected or realized mean return. The larger this coefficient is, the greater the dispersion of values as a proportion of the expected or realized mean return. (See the formula in the Appendix.)

Example: Calculate the coefficient of variation of the mean return from the preceding example.

Keystrokes	Display	Comment
.0924 ENTER	0.0924	Enters the standard deviation.
.1220 ÷	0.7574	Coefficient of variation.

*Note that it is necessary to calculate the mean before calculating the standard deviation.

BETA COEFFICIENT

The beta coefficient, sometimes called simply *beta,* is a widely used measure of market risk. The term *market risk* refers to the dispersion of values around the mean value that are caused by general fluctuations in the general stock market. Beta thus describes the sensitivity of the return of a particular stock or portfolio of stocks to the return of the market as measured by, for example, the Standard & Poor's 500 Stock Index.

A beta of 1.0 indicates that a stock's rate of return corresponds closely to the return of the market. A beta of less than 1.0 reveals that the stock's return fluctuates less than the return of the market, and a beta of more than 1.0, that it fluctuates more. For example, if the S&P 500 return is 10 percent, a stock with a beta of 1.0 will have, on the average, a return of 10 percent; a stock with a beta of 0.6 will have a return of about 6 percent; and a stock with a beta of 1.3 will have a return of about 13 percent.

Beta is defined as the quotient of the covariance of a stock's return movements with the market's return movements in relation to the variance of the market's returns. (Also see the formulas in the Appendix.)

$$\text{Beta} = \frac{\text{covariance of a stock and the market}}{\text{variance of the market}}$$

The following program can be used to calculate the beta coefficient of a stock or a portfolio of stocks.

KEYSTROKES	DISPLAY		KEYSTROKES	DISPLAY	
f P/R			Σ+	22-	49
f CLEAR PRGM	00-		g s	23-	43 48
Σ+	01-	49	R/S	24-	31
g GTO 00	02-	43,33 00	x><y	25-	34
g s	03-	43 48	R/S	26-	31
x	04-	20	R↓	27-	33
ENTER	05-	36	2	28-	2
g ŷ,r	06-	43 2	yˣ	29-	21
R↓	07-	33	RCL 7	30-	45 7
x	08-	20	x><y	31-	34
RCL 1	09-	45 1	÷	32-	10
1	10-	1	STO .0	33-	44 48 0
−	11-	30	R/S	34-	31
RCL 1	12-	45 1	RCL 8	35-	45 8
÷	13-	10	x	36-	20
x	14-	20	RCL 9	37-	45 9
STO 7	15-	44 7	x><y	38-	34
R/S	16-	31	−	39-	30
g x̄	17-	43 0	STO 0	40-	44 0
STO 8	18-	44 8	R/S	41-	31
x><y	19-	34	g x̂,r	42-	43 1
STO 9	20-	44 9	x><y	43-	34
x><y	21-	34	2	44-	2

KEYSTROKES	DISPLAY		KEYSTROKES	DISPLAY	
y^x	45-	21	x	54-	20
R/S	46-	31	-	55-	30
RCL 5	47-	45 5	RCL 1	56-	45 1
RCL 0	48-	45 0	3	57-	3
RCL 4	49-	45 4	-	58-	30
x	50-	20	÷	59-	10
-	51-	30	g √x	60-	43 21
RCL .0	52-	45 48 0	g GTO 00	61-	43,33 00
RCL 6	53-	45 6	f P/R		

REGISTERS*			
n: Unused	i: Unused	PV: Unused	PMT: Unused
FV: Unused	R_0: Alpha	R_1: n	R_2: Σx
R_3: Σx^2	R_4: Σy	R_5: Σy^2	R_6: Σxy
R_7: Covariance	R_8: Mean x	R_9: Mean y	$R_{.0}$: Beta
$R_{.1}$: Unused			

*The content of registers R_1 through R_6 changes after the standard deviation is calculated.

The calculations may be made as follows:

1. Key in the program.
2. Press f CLEAR REG.
3. For each input pair of values, key in the dependent or y value and press ENTER; then key in the corresponding independent or x value and press R/S.

4. After all data pairs are keyed in, press [g] [GTO] 03 [R/S] to obtain the covariance.

5. Press [R/S] to obtain the standard deviation of the independent or x variable.

6. Press [R/S] to obtain the standard deviation of the dependent or y variable.

7. Press [R/S] to obtain the beta coefficient.

Example: The rate of return on Winst & Prat's stock and on the Standard & Poor's 500 Stock Index has been as shown in the table below.

Year	S&P 500	Winst & Prat
1	.124	.172
2	.135	.194
3	.067	.165
4	−.082	−.130
5	.079	.094
6	.190	.213
7	.210	.244

What is Winst & Prat's beta?*

*Remember to enter first the dependent or y variable—in this example, the return for Winst & Prat.

Keystrokes	Display	Comment
f CLEAR REG		
.172 ENTER .124 R/S	1.00	
.194 ENTER .135 R/S	2.00	
.165 ENTER .067 R/S	3.00	
.130 CHS ENTER .082 CHS R/S	4.00	
.094 ENTER .079 R/S	5.00	
.213 ENTER .190 R/S	6.00	
.244 ENTER .210 R/S	7.00	Total number of entries.
g GTO 03 R/S	0.01	Covariance.
R/S	0.09	Standard deviation of the independent variable.
R/S	0.12	Standard deviation of the dependent variable.
R/S	1.24	Beta coefficient.

In addition to the beta coefficient, you may want to determine the alpha coefficient, the coefficient of determination, and the standard error of estimate.

Alpha is the return obtained from the stock (or portfolio) independently of the return on the market index. It represents the rate of return you would obtain from the stock (or portfolio) if the rate of return on the S&P 500 were zero. The *coefficient of determination,* on the other hand, measures how good beta is as a predictor of future return movements. (The coefficient of determination is equal to the coefficient of correlation *squared*.) It reveals the percentage of variation in a stock's rate of return that is explained by the variation in the market's rate of return. A coefficient of 1.00 would indicate that changes in the market would explain 100 percent of the changes in the stock's return. A coefficient of 0.00 would indicate that the market would not explain the stock's return movements at all. (See the formulas in the Appendix.)

The *standard error of the estimate* is the standard deviation of the data values around the calculated regression line. The larger it is, the larger the dispersion. In general, about 68 percent of the single-period return values are within 1 plus and minus standard deviations of the mean return; 95 percent within 2 plus and minus standard deviations; and 99 percent within 3 plus and minus standard deviations. (See the formula in the Appendix.)

The previous program can calculate both of these coefficients, as follows:

Keystrokes	Display	Comment
R/S	0.01	Alpha coefficient.
R/S	0.91	Coefficient of determination.
R/S	0.04	Standard error of the estimate.

This program also calculates the arithmetic mean for both series of data, as follows:

Keystrokes	Display	Comment
RCL 8	0.10	Mean return of the S&P 500.
RCL 9	0.14	Mean return of Winst & Prat.

Despite beta's popularity in the investment community, beta poses some problems. Among them are:

1. A company's historical beta may not be the same as its future beta.
2. Different betas can be obtained depending upon the number of time periods observed and the length of the time intervals used.

The beta and alpha coefficients may also be calculated on the basis of *excess* or *risk premium* rates of return for the Standard

& Poor's 500 Stock Index, individual stocks, or portfolios. Chapter 6, Portfolio Management, presents applications in which the excess rate of return may be used.

The excess rate of return or risk premium is simply the difference between the rate of return of common stocks and the risk-free rate of return. The risk-free rate of return is frequently measured by the 3-month U.S. Treasury Bill rate.

To calculate the beta and alpha coefficients and the related statistics of time series on the basis of excess rates of return, proceed as follows:

1. Subtract the risk-free rate of return from every data value in both time series.
2. Use the program on pages 12 and 13.

REFERENCES

1. Jerome L. Valentine and Edmund A. Mennis, *Quantitative Techniques for Financial Analysis*, rev. ed. (Richard D. Irwin, Homewood, Ill., 1980), chap. 7.
2. Charles A. D'Ambrosio, *Principles of Modern Investments* (Science Research Associates, Chicago, 1976), chap. 16.

Section
1-3
STOCK VALUATION MODELS

A great number of stock valuation models have appeared in the finance literature. Given certain assumptions, these models estimate the intrinsic or theoretical value of securities. If the value derived from these models is greater than the current market value, the stock is said to be undervalued and therefore should be bought. If, on the other hand, the intrinsic value is smaller than the current market value, the stock is overvalued and therefore should be sold.

The basic idea behind these models is that stock prices, over the long run, tend to converge toward their intrinsic value. Thus, by identifying over- and undervalued stocks, above-average rates of return can be obtained.

Of the innumerable models that have been developed, four models are presented here. These models have sound theoretical support and are widely used by analysts.

PRESENT-VALUE MODEL

The *present-value model* discounts future cash flows at a hurdle rate or rate of return. The present value of future cash flows represents the maximum price that can be paid to realize the desired or hurdle rate of return.

The difference between the discounted future cash flows or present value and the initial cash investment is the net present value of the investment. When the net present value is positive, the rate of return earned on the investment will be greater than the hurdle rate. On the contrary, when the net present value is negative, the rate of return earned on the investment will be smaller than the hurdle rate.

The HP-12C "Owner's Handbook and Problem-Solving Guide" (pages 65–71) explains how to calculate the net present value of an investment.

Example: Wirtz & Williston's common stock is selling for $18 a share. You expect to receive $1.10, $1.65, and $1.85 in dividends during the next 3 years and then sell the stock for $29½. What are the present and the net present values of your investment if you require a minimum return of 15 percent?

Keystrokes	Display	Comment
f CLEAR REG	0.00	Clears financial and storage registers.
0 CHS g CFo	0.00	
1.10 g CFj	1.10	Enters dividend first year.
1.65 g CFj	1.65	Enters dividend second year.
1.85 ENTER 29.5 + g CFj	31.35	Enters dividend third year plus selling price.
15 i	15.00	Enters discount rate.
f NPV	22.82	Present value.
18 −	4.82	Net present value.

Since the net present value is positive, the return you will obtain by investing in this stock will be greater than 15 percent. Thus, according to this model, you should buy the stock now.

GRAHAM AND DODD'S MODEL

Graham and Dodd's stock valuation model is stated in terms of the actual earnings per share available for common stock, E, the expected annual growth rate in earnings, G, and the yield on high-grade corporate bonds, AAA. According to this model, the value of a common stock share, V, is given by the equation

$$V = E \times (8.5 + 2G) \left(\frac{4.4}{\text{AAA}}\right)$$

The basic assumption of this model is that stock prices are related directly to earnings growth and indirectly to yields on high-grade corporate bonds. The rationale is that when yields on AAA bonds rise, investors switch from the stock market to the bond market. And as investors sell their stock positions, stock prices decline.

Example: The earnings per share of Graham's common stock is $4.17 and the expected annual growth rate of earnings is 9 percent. If AAA bonds are selling to yield 14 percent, what is the value of Graham's common stock?

Keystrokes	Display	Comment
4.17 [ENTER]	4.17	Enters earnings per share.
8.5 [ENTER]	8.50	
2 [ENTER] 9 [×] [+]	26.50	
4.4 [ENTER] 14 [÷] [×]	8.33	Earnings multiplier.
[×]	34.73	Value of a common stock share.

REFERENCE

Benjamin Graham, "The Decade 1965–1974: Its Significance for Financial Analysis," in *The Renaissance of Value* (Financial Analysts Research Foundation, Charlottesville, Va., 1974), pp. 2–12.

GORDON'S CONSTANT-DIVIDEND GROWTH MODEL

Gordon's constant-dividend growth model is similar to the present-value model. In both models, future cash flows are discounted at a minimum required rate of return. Gordon's model, however, introduces several additional assumptions. These assumptions are:

- Dividends, D, will be growing forever at a constant rate of growth, g.
- The time period is infinity.
- The dividends growth rate, g, is smaller than the minimum required rate of return, k.

Based on this assumption, Gordon developed the following formula to determine the price, P_0, for which a stock should sell.

$$P_0 = \frac{D_1}{k - g}$$

where D_1 is the dividend to be received next period; D_1 is equal to $D_0(1 + g)$.*

Example: Gordon & Gordon Corporation has paid \$2.25 in dividends over the past 12 months. Dividends have been growing during the last 15 years at an average annual rate of 9 percent, and you expect this trend to continue. Assuming your required rate of return is 14 percent, how much should you be willing to pay for 1 share of Gordon & Gordon's stock?

*Note that k and g should be entered in decimal form, e.g., 15 percent would be 0.15.

Keystrokes	Display	Comment
2.25 ENTER	2.25	Enters D_0.
1 ENTER .09 +	1.09	
×	2.45	D_1.
.14 ENTER .09 −	0.05	
÷	49.05	P_0.

Thus, according to this model, the intrinsic value of Gordon & Gordon's stock is $49.05.

HOLT'S GROWTH DURATION MODEL

Holt's growth duration model determines the minimum length of time during which an above-average rate of growth in earnings per share for a growth stock must be maintained in order to justify the stock's current market price. This model assumes that the risk relationship between a growth stock and the S&P 500 Stock Index (or other broad market index) remains the same over time. Based on this assumption and by examining the differential earnings growth rates and current price/earning (P/E) ratios of the growth stock and the S&P 500, it is possible to compute the duration, T, of earnings growth for the growth stock implied by the current market price. (See the formula in the Appendix.)

The following HP-12C program calculates the implied earnings growth duration, T, for the growth stock analyzed.

KEYSTROKES	DISPLAY	KEYSTROKES	DISPLAY
f P/R		RCL 2	13- 45 2
f CLEAR PRGM	00-	+	14- 40
÷	01- 10	RCL 4	15- 45 4
g LN	02- 43 23	+	16- 40
1	03- 1	÷	17- 10
0	04- 0	g LN	18- 43 23
g LN	05- 43 23	1	19- 1
÷	06- 10	0	20- 0
1	07- 1	g LN	21- 43 23
RCL 1	08- 45 1	÷	22- 10
+	09- 40	÷	23- 10
RCL 3	10- 45 3	g GTO 00	24- 43,33 00
+	11- 40	f P/R	
1	12- 1		

REGISTERS			
n: Unused	i: Unused	PV: Unused	PMT: Unused
FV: Unused	R_0: Unused	R_1: Δ Eg	R_2: Δ Ea
R_3: Dg	R_4: Da	R_5–R_6: Unused	

The calculations may be made as follows:

1. Key in the program and press f CLEAR REG.
2. Key in the earnings growth rate of the growth stock, Δ Eg, and press STO 1.

3. Key in the earnings growth rate of the market index, ΔEa, and press [STO] 2.

4. Key in the dividend yield of the growth stock, Dg, and press [STO] 3.

5. Key in the dividend yield of the market index, Da, and press [STO] 4.

6. Key in the P/E ratio of the growth stock, press [ENTER], key in the P/E ratio of the market index, and press [R/S].

7. For a new case, press [f] CLEAR [REG] and go to step 2.

Example: You have the following data for Apple Bites Technologies, a growth stock, and the S&P 500:

	APPLE BITES TECHNOLOGIES	S&P 500
P/E ratio	18.00	8.30
Earnings growth rate	0.15	0.08
Current dividend yield	0.06	0.07

What is the implied earnings growth rate duration for Apple Bites Technologies?

Keystrokes	Display	Comment
[f] CLEAR [REG]		Clears registers.
.15 [STO] 1	0.15	Enters ΔEg.
.08 [STO] 2	0.08	Enters ΔEa.
.06 [STO] 3	0.06	Enters Dg.
.07 [STO] 4	0.07	Enters Da.
18 [ENTER] 8.3	8.3	Enters P/E ratios.
[R/S]	15.22	Implied earnings growth rate duration.

The implied duration of the earnings growth rate is 15.22 years. That is, to justify Apple Bites Technologies' present P/E ratio, earnings have to keep growing during the next 15.22 years at an annual rate of 15 percent. After this period, the model assumes the earnings growth rate will decline to a level equal to that of the S&P 500.

If you think that the company will enjoy an earnings growth rate higher than 15 percent during the next 15.22 years or that it will be able to maintain the 15 percent earnings growth rate for a period longer than 15.22 years, you may consider investing in this stock. If your forecast is right, the price of Apple Bites Technologies should increase.

REFERENCE

Frank K. Reilly, *Investment Analysis and Portfolio Management,* 2d ed. (Dryden Press, Hinsdale, Ill., 1985), chap. 10.

Section
1-4
OTHER MEASUREMENTS

ADJUSTMENTS FOR STOCK SPLITS AND STOCK DIVIDENDS

A stock split consists of a reduction in the par or book value of a stock and a consequent increase in the number of shares outstanding. A company declaring a 2 for 1 split would end up with a stock par value half the presplit par value and with twice as many shares.

A stock dividend, on the other hand, is simply a distribution of retained earnings in the form of stock. A stockholder owning 100 shares and receiving a 5 percent stock dividend would end up with 105 shares.

Regardless of how favorable these stock splits and stock dividends are, a problem arises when comparing per-share financial data before and after the stock split or stock dividend. In order to make per-share financial data comparable, all past data have to be adjusted.

Presplit or prestock dividend data have to be divided by 1 plus the percentage stock dividend or split.

Example: The earnings per share (EPS) for the EZ Corporation from 1980 through 1985 are as shown below.

YEAR	EPS
1980	1.50
1981	1.80
1982	1.76
1983	1.94
1984	2.16
1985	3.08

In January 1986, a 2 for 1 stock split was declared. What are the adjusted earnings per share for 1980 through 1985?*

Keystrokes	Display	Comment
1.50 ENTER	1.50	
1 ENTER 1 +	2.00	Adjustment factor.
÷	0.75	Adjusted EPS for 1980.
1.80 g LST × ÷	0.90	Adjusted EPS for 1981.
1.76 g LST × ÷	0.88	Adjusted EPS for 1982.
1.94 g LST × ÷	0.97	Adjusted EPS for 1983.
2.16 g LST × ÷	1.08	Adjusted EPS for 1984.
3.08 g LST × ÷	1.54	Adjusted EPS for 1985.

In July 1986, the company declares a 5 percent stock dividend. What are the readjusted EPS for 1980 through 1985?†

*This stock split increased the number of shares by 100 percent. Thus, you have to add 1 to the denominator, which is the decimal form for 100 percent.

†Remember to use the EPS adjusted for the stock split in January 1986.

Keystrokes	Display	Comment
.75 [ENTER]	0.75	
1 [ENTER] .05 [+]	1.05	Adjustment factor.
[÷]	0.71	Readjusted EPS for 1980.
.90 [g] [LST ×] [÷]	0.86	Readjusted EPS for 1981.
.88 [g] [LST ×] [÷]	0.84	Readjusted EPS for 1982.
.97 [g] [LST ×] [÷]	0.92	Readjusted EPS for 1983.
1.08 [g] [LST ×] [÷]	1.03	Readjusted EPS for 1984.
1.54 [g] [LST ×] [÷]	1.47	Readjusted EPS for 1985.

WEIGHTED-AVERAGE NUMBER OF SHARES

The weighted-average number of shares outstanding constitutes the basis for all the financial data reported on a per-share basis—for example, earnings per share.

In calculating the weighted-average number of shares outstanding, reacquired and issued shares have to be weighted according to the period of time during which they were outstanding. As stock dividends, stock splits, and reverse splits alter the number of shares outstanding, they too have to be taken into account. Use of the [g] [Δ DYS] function of the HP-12C greatly simplifies the calculation of the weighted-average number of shares. To calculate the weighted-average number of shares outstanding during a designated period of time, proceed as follows:

1. Key in the number of shares outstanding at the beginning of the period and press [STO] 1.
2. Key in the number of shares subsequently issued or retired, press [CHS] if shares were retired, and press [ENTER].
3. Key in the date (MM.DDYYYY) on which shares were issued or retired and press [ENTER].

4. Key in the date (MM.DDYYYY) after the end of the period and press $\boxed{g}$ $\boxed{\Delta \text{ DYS}}$.*

5. Key in the number of days in the period and press $\boxed{\div}$ $\boxed{x><y}$ $\boxed{R\downarrow}$ $\boxed{x}$ $\boxed{\text{STO}}$ $\boxed{+}$ 1.

6. Repeat steps 2 through 5 for more shares, issues, and repurchases.

7. Press $\boxed{\text{RCL}}$ 1 to find the weighted average number of shares.

Example: WASO Corporation had 20,000 common shares outstanding on January 1, 1987, and issued 4000 common shares on March 17. On November 1, WASO repurchased 3200 common shares. What is WASO Corporation's weighted-average number of shares outstanding during 1987?

Keystrokes	Display	Comment
20000 $\boxed{\text{STO}}$ 1	20000.00	Enters shares outstanding at the beginning of the year.
4000 $\boxed{\text{ENTER}}$	4000.00	Enters shares issued on March 17.
3.171987 $\boxed{\text{ENTER}}$	3.17	
1.011988 $\boxed{g}$ $\boxed{\Delta \text{ DYS}}$	290.00	Number of days outstanding.
365 $\boxed{\div}$ $\boxed{x><y}$ $\boxed{R\downarrow}$ $\boxed{x}$ $\boxed{\text{STO}}$ $\boxed{+}$ 1	3178.08	
3200 $\boxed{\text{CHS}}$ $\boxed{\text{ENTER}}$	−3200.00	Enters shares repurchased on November 1.
11.011987 $\boxed{\text{ENTER}}$	11.02	
1.011988 $\boxed{g}$ $\boxed{\Delta \text{ DYS}}$	61.00	Number of days outstanding.
365 $\boxed{\div}$ $\boxed{x><y}$ $\boxed{R\downarrow}$ $\boxed{x}$ $\boxed{\text{STO}}$ $\boxed{+}$ 1	−534.79	
$\boxed{\text{RCL}}$ 1	22643.29	Weighted-average number of shares outstanding.

*The day after the end of the year is taken instead of the last day of the year in order to include the shares outstanding the last day of the year. If the last day of the year were chosen, it would be excluded from the calculations.

The following program can be used to calculate the weighted-average number of shares outstanding.

KEYSTROKES	DISPLAY		KEYSTROKES	DISPLAY	
f P/R			÷	06-	10
f CLEAR PRGM	00-		RCL 1	07-	45 1
STO 1	01-	44 1	x	08-	20
x><y	02-	34	STO + 4	09- 44	40 4
RCL 2	03-	45 2	RCL 4	10-	45 4
g Δ DYS	04-	43 26	g GTO 00	11-	43,33 00
RCL 3	05-	45 3	f P/R		

REGISTERS			
n: Unused	i: Unused	PV: Unused	PMT: Unused
FV: Unused	R_0: Unused	R_1: Used	R_2: Day after end of period
R_3: Number of days in the period	R_4: Weighted-average number of shares	R_5–R_8: Unused	

The calculations may be made as follows:

1. Key in the program.

2. Press f CLEAR REG.

3. Key in the date (MM.DDYYYY) after the end of the period and press STO 2.

4. Key in the number of days in the period and press STO 3.

5. Key in the date (MM.DDYYYY) that corresponds to the beginning of the period, press ENTER, key in the number of shares outstanding, and press R/S.

6. Key in the next date (MM.DDYYYY) at which shares were either issued or repurchased, press ENTER, key in the number of shares,* and press R/S.

7. Repeat step **6** for all stock issues or repurchases.

8. For a new case, return to step 2.

Keystrokes	Display	Comment
1.011988 STO 2	1.01	Day after the end of the year.
365 STO 3	365.00	Number of days in the period.
1.011987 ENTER	1.01	
20000 R/S	20000.00	
3.171987 ENTER	3.17	
4000 R/S	23178.08	
11.011987 ENTER	11.01	
3200 CHS R/S	22643.29	Weighted-average number of shares outstanding.

REFERENCE

Donald E. Kieso and Jerry J. Weygandt, *Intermediate Accounting*, 3d ed. (John Wiley & Sons, New York, 1980), pp. 732–734.

MARGIN REQUIREMENTS

The term *margin requirements* refers to the limits the Federal Reserve imposes on the amount investors can borrow from their brokers or other lenders to finance stock investments.

*Don't forget to press CHS if shares were repurchased.

In analyzing margin requirements, we have to differentiate between "long" and "short" positions. Investors are said to have a "long position" if they have purchased stock, whereas they are said to have a "short position" if they have sold securities they do not own yet—that is, securities they have borrowed.

Margin Requirements on Long Positions

An investor's *margin* is the percent of his or her equity in relation to the current market value of the securities held.

The equity is the difference between the current market value of the securities held and the amount owed to the broker.

Example: If you have $3500 worth of securities and you owe your broker $900, what are your equity and margin?

Keystrokes	Display	Comment
3500 [ENTER] [ENTER]	3500.00	Enters market value of your stock.
900 [−]	2600.00	Your equity.
[%T]	74.29	Your margin.

Initial Margin. The term *initial margin* refers to the margin an investor has to maintain initially when purchasing securities. Given an initial margin requirement, the maximum amount of stock that can be purchased, I, is:

$$I = \frac{\text{equity}}{\text{margin requirement}}$$

Example: What is the maximum amount of stock you can buy if you have $2600 and the initial margin requirement is 60 percent?

Keystrokes	Display	Comment
2600 ENTER ENTER	2600.00	Enters your equity.
.60 ÷	4333.33	Your maximum investment.
−	−1733.33	Dollar amount you can borrow.

Maintenance Margin.   After the day the securities are purchased, a different margin requirement applies. This new margin requirement is called the *maintenance margin.*

When the market value of the securities falls and the maintenance margin level is reached, the investor will receive a "margin call" from the broker asking for more money. To calculate this level, use the following formula:

$$\text{Market value of securities} = \frac{\text{amount borrowed from broker}}{1 - \text{maintenance margin}}$$

Example 1:   If the maintenance margin your broker requires is 30 percent, when will you receive a "margin call"?

Keystrokes	Display	Comment
900 ENTER	900.00	Enters amount you owe your broker.
1 ENTER .30 − ÷	1285.71	Market value below which you will receive a margin call.

Example 2:   If the market value of your securities increases to $4800, what will be your margin and the limit of your investment? By how much can the value of your stock drop before you get a margin call?

Keystrokes	Display	Comment
4800 [ENTER] [ENTER]	4800.00	Enters market value of your stock.
900 [−] [STO 1]	3900.00	Your equity.
[%T]	81.25	Your margin.
[RCL] 1 .60 [÷]	6500.00	Limit of your investment.
4800 [ENTER] 1285.71 [Δ%]	−73.21	Percentage decline before you receive a margin call.

Margin Requirements on Short Positions

Initial Margin. The initial margin requirements for short positions are normally equal to those of long positions. To calculate the initial margin, just multiply the value of the securities sold short by the initial margin requirements.

Example: If you sell short stocks worth $4000 and the initial margin requirement is 60 percent, how much money do you have to put up?

Keystrokes	Display	Comment
4000 [ENTER] [ENTER]	4000.00	Enters market value of stocks you sold short.
.60 [×]	2400.00	Minimum initial margin.
[−]	1600.00	Amount you may borrow.

Once you have calculated the initial margin, you can determine the margin of your account by using the formula

$$\text{Margin} = \frac{\text{initial margin} + \dfrac{\text{initial value}}{\text{of stocks}} - \dfrac{\text{actual market}}{\text{value of stocks}}}{\text{actual market value of stocks}}$$

Example: If the value of the stocks you sold short goes down to $3800, what is your margin?

Keystrokes	Display	Comment
2400 [ENTER]	2400.00	Enters your initial margin.
4000 [+] 3800 [−]	2600.00	Your equity.
[g] [LST x] [x><y] [%T]	68.42	Your actual margin.

Maintenance Margin. In the case of short positions, an investor will receive a "margin call" when the market value of the stocks sold short goes above a certain level. This level can be calculated as follows:

$$\text{Market value} = \frac{\text{initial proceeds} + \text{initial margin}}{1 - \text{maintenance margin}}$$

Example: Using the data of the previous examples, when will you receive a margin call if your broker requires a 40 percent maintenance margin on short positions?

Keystrokes	Display	Comment
4000 [ENTER]	4000.00	Enters initial proceeds.
2400 [+]	6400.00	
1 [ENTER] .40 [+] [÷]	10666.67	Market value above which you will receive a margin call.

REFERENCE

James W. Jenkins, "Self-Correcting Problems in Investment Management" (Allyn & Bacon, Boston, 1974), chap. 4.

RIGHTS OFFERINGS

A *rights offering* is an option to buy a predetermined number of shares at a specified subscription price. Normally, this subscription price is lower than the current market price of the stock. Rights are offered to existing shareholders by corporations issuing new common stock. In a rights offering, each shareholder receives one right for every share of stock owned.

To calculate the number of new shares to which a shareholder has a right to subscribe, divide the number of shares a shareholder owns by the number of rights necessary to subscribe to one share of the new stock.

Example: Ms. Pierce owns 250 shares of a corporation that is issuing new common stock. If 10 rights are required to buy one new share, how many shares of stock can Ms. Pierce buy with her 250 rights?

Keystrokes	Display	Comment
250 [ENTER]	250.00	Enters number of rights.
10 [÷]	25.00	Shares of new common stock.

To calculate the value of a right, we have to consider whether the stock to which it is attached is selling "cum rights" or "ex rights."

If the market price of the stock includes the value of the rights to be received, the stock sells cum rights; otherwise, it sells ex rights. Normally, the new shareholder receives the rights if the stock is sold before the ex rights date, and the old shareholder receives the rights if it is sold on or after this date.

Value of a Right, Cum Rights.   The value of one right, cum rights, is given by the formula

$$\text{Value of one right, cum rights} = \frac{\text{market price of stock, cum rights} - \text{subscription price}}{\text{number of rights required to purchase one new share} + 1}$$

Example: The stock Ms. Pierce owns is selling, cum rights, for $110 a share, and the subscription price is $90. What is the value of each right?

Keystrokes	Display	Comment
110 [ENTER]	110.00	Enters market price of stock, cum rights.
90 [−]	20.00	
10 [ENTER] 1 [+] [÷]	1.82	Value of each right, cum rights.

Value of a Right, Ex Rights.   The value of one right, ex rights, is given by the formula

$$\text{Value of one right, ex rights} = \frac{\text{market price of stock, ex rights} - \text{subscription price}}{\text{number of rights required to purchase one new share}}$$

Example: What will be the value of each right if the stock Ms. Pierce owns sells, ex rights, for $108.20?

Keystrokes	Display	Comment
108.2 [ENTER]	108.20	Enters market price of stock, ex rights.
90 [−]	18.20	
10 [÷]	1.82	Value of each right, ex rights.

REFERENCE

J. Fred Weston and Eugene F. Brigham, *Managerial Finance*, 7th ed.
(Dryden Press, Hinsdale, Ill., 1981), pp. 761–765.

TREND ANALYSIS

Trend analysis is the study of the direction of a time series. A
time series is a set of quantitative data taken at regular
consecutive time intervals, e.g., weeks, months, or years.

Statistical analysis of trends in time series is particularly
important to financial analysts. Important and frequently used
data such as earnings and dividends per share, price, and
dividend yields are presented as time series. Analysis of these
trends and other time series may provide analysts with valuable
insights.

The HP-12C "Solutions Handbook" presents several programs
that facilitate the use of sophisticated statistical tools in
forecasting and analyzing trends, such as moving averages (pages
70–79); Gompertz curve trend analysis (pages 79–83);
exponential smoothing forecasts (pages 83–87); and exponential,
logarithmic, and power curve fitting (pages 94–101). The
HP-12C "Owners Handbook and Problem-Solving Guide" also
contains interesting programs, such as linear estimation (page
91).

The particular trend analysis tool to be used depends on the
historical or expected pattern that can be detected on the time
series to be analyzed. The moving-averages programs can provide
a good start in analyzing trends. Moving averages, by
eliminating short-term erratic fluctuations, permit medium- and
long-term trends and patterns to become more easily noticeable.

Not all time series, however, have a clear trend. Stock price
movements, for example, are frequently random in the short

run—several weeks. In such a case, no significant trend analysis can be performed.

If a trend becomes noticeable, the following techniques can be used:

- Linear trends: linear estimation
- S-shaped trends: Gompertz curve trend analysis
- Exponential trends: exponential curve fit

Conversion of time series into logarithmic time series may prove to be very helpful, particularly in studying growth patterns. The variable being examined can easily be converted into natural or common logarithms by using the HP-12C [g] [LN] function.

BONDS

Section
2-1
RETURN
MEASUREMENTS

NOMINAL YIELD

The *nominal yield* is the coupon rate a bond carries. The nominal yield of a bond issued with a 12 percent coupon rate, for example, is 12 percent. This yield is the expected rate of return based on the bond's par value.

CURRENT YIELD

The *current yield* relates the coupon interest payments of a bond to its current market price. The current yield is thus a measure of the cash income a bond offers at the current market price.

Example: A 12 percent coupon rate bond is selling for $910.00. What is its current yield?

Keystrokes	Display	Comment
120 [ENTER]	120.00	Enters coupon payments.
910	910.00	Enters current market price.
[÷] 100 [x]	13.19	Current yield.

YIELD TO MATURITY

The *yield to maturity* is the rate of return an investor will realize by buying a bond at current market price and holding it to maturity. The yield to maturity is simply an internal rate of return that equates the price paid for the bond to the future stream of coupon and principal receipts.

An important reinvestment assumption implicit in yield to maturity calculations is that the investor will be able to reinvest the coupon payments at an average rate of return equal to the computed yield to maturity. Whenever this assumption is violated, the realized yield will differ from the computed yield to maturity.

The HP-12C has a function, f YTM, that greatly simplifies the calculation of the yield to maturity.

Example: You are considering buying a bond just issued by Aut-O-Matic, Inc. The characteristics of the bond are:

Today's date	January 1, 1985
Redemption date	January 1, 1990
Par value	$1000
Coupon rate	14 percent payable semiannually
Coupon payments	$70 twice a year
Quoted price	$920

What is the yield to maturity on this bond?

Keystrokes	Display	Comment
f CLEAR FIN	0.00	Clears financial registers.
92 PV	92.00	Enters quoted price (as a percentage of par value).
14 PMT	14.00	Enters coupon rate.
1.011985 ENTER	1.011985	Enters purchase date.
1.011990	1.011990	Enters maturity date.
f YTM	16.41	Yield to maturity.

The after-tax yield to maturity can easily be calculated using the HP-12C "After-Tax Yield" program (HP-12C "Solutions Handbook," pages 65–67). Another HP-12C program, "30/360 Day Basis Bonds" (HP-12C "Owners Handbook and Problem-Solving Guide," pages 182–185), can also be used to calculate the yield to maturity. This program calculates the yield to maturity of semiannual coupon bonds on the basis of 30-day months and 360-day years.

For bonds with annual coupon payments, the HP-12C "Annual Coupon Bonds" program (HP-12C "Owner's Handbook and Problem-Solving Guide," pages 185–187) can be used to calculate the yield to maturity.

YIELD TO CALL DATE

Frequently, bond indentures contain some type of call provision. Most call provisions entitle the issuing company to call in the bonds for redemption before their maturity. The price at which the company can redeem the bonds is known as the *call price* and is frequently equal to the par value of the bond plus a call premium.

When bonds trade at prices equal to or above their call prices, it is possible that the company will call in the bonds for redemption. Under these circumstances, the yield to call date provides a more meaningful measure of the bond's expected return than does the yield to maturity. The yield to call date assumes that the bond will not remain outstanding until maturity but rather will be retired at the end of the call date.

The calculation of the yield to call date is similar to the calculation of the yield to maturity. The only differences are that, in calculating the yield to call date, the investment horizon extends only to the call date, and the redemption value is not the par value but the call price.

In calculating the yield to call date with the Hp-12C, the ⨎ IRR function, rather than the ⨎ YTM function, has to be used. Since the ⨎ YTM function assumes that the redemption value is equal to the par value, the use of this function does not take into account the premium received when the bond is called in for redemption.

Example: Assuming that Aut-O-Matic's bonds are callable after 2 years at 114 ($1140) and that they are trading at $920, calculate the expected yield to call date.*

---

*As coupon payments are received twice a year, the compounding period that should be used is 6 months. The yield to maturity so obtained will be the semiannual rate of return. To convert it to an annual basis, simply multiply it by 2.

Keystrokes	Display	Comment
f CLEAR FIN	0.00	Clears financial registers.
920 CHS g CFo.	−920.00	Enters quoted price.
70 g CFj.	70.00	Enters semiannual interest payments.
3 g Nj	3.00	Enters number of periods during which only semiannual interest will be received.
1140 ENTER	1140.00	Enters call price.
70 + g CFj	1210.00	Call price plus accrued semiannual interest for the last period.
f IRR	12.57	
2 x	25.14	Yield to call date.

REALIZED COMPOUND YIELD

The realized compound yield measures the yield an investor has been able to obtain by investing in bonds. This measure takes into account the average rate at which the investor has been able to reinvest the coupon payments.

As already indicated, the yield to maturity and the yield to call date assume that the investor is able to reinvest interim cash flows at the computed yield. This assumption, however, can distort the real rate of return earned on the initial investment if the bond was purchased during a period of particularly high interest rates or if the interest income was spent and not reinvested. It is, thus, necessary to modify the calculation of the yield to maturity in such a way that the average rate at which cash flows are reinvested can be taken into consideration.

The HP-12C "Modified Internal Rate of Return" program (HP-12C "Owners Handbook and Problem-Solving Guide," pages 167–168) can be used to determine the realized compound yield.

Example: Calculate the realized compound yield you would expect if you bought the 5-year Aut-O-Matic bond at a price of $920, held it to maturity, and reinvested the coupon payments at an average rate of 10 percent.

Keystrokes	Display	Comment
f CLEAR FIN	0.00	Clears financial registers.
0 g CFo	0.00	
70 g CFj	70.00	Enters semiannual interest payments.
9 g Nj	9.00	Enters number of periods during which only semiannual interest will be received.
1070 g CFj	1070.00	Enters par value plus accrued semiannual interest for the last period.
10 ENTER 2 ÷ i	5.00	Enters semiannual reinvestment rate.
f NPV	1154.43	Present value of cash in-flows.
CHS PV	−1154.43	
10 n	10.00	Enters number of periods.
FV	1880.45	Future value of cash in-flows.
920 CHS PV	−920.00	Enters purchase price.
i	7.41	Semiannual realized compound yield.
2 x	14.82	Realized compound yield.

EQUIVALENT YIELDS ON TAX-EXEMPT SECURITIES

Certain bond issues, like municipal bonds, are tax-exempt; that is, the interest income they provide is exempt from federal income taxes. Only the capital gains or losses are subject to federal taxation. The yield to maturity of these tax-exempt issues has to be restated on a before-tax basis to make it comparable to the yield of other, fully taxable bond issues. This is usually done by computing what is known as the *fully taxable equivalent yield* (FTEY). The FTEY is the yield to maturity that fully taxable bond issues have to offer in order to provide a rate of return equivalent to that obtained by investing in a tax-exempt issue.

The FTEY for securities selling at par value is found by dividing the tax-exempt yield by 1 minus the marginal tax bracket of the investor.

Example: What is the fully taxable equivalent yield of an 8 percent municipal bond selling at par value? Assume your marginal tax bracket is 38 percent.

Keystrokes	Display	Comment
8 [ENTER]	8.00	Enters coupon rate.
1 [ENTER] .38 [−] [÷]	12.90	FTEY.

YIELD ON ZERO-COUPON BONDS

Zero-coupon bonds are pure discount bonds with no coupon payments at all. Since these deeply discounted bonds don't pay interest regularly, their entire return is derived from the discount. In addition, they are free of reinvestment risks; there are no cash flows to reinvest. Thus, the promised yield or yield to maturity is equal to the realized compound yield.

The HP-12C [f] [PRICE] and [f] [YTM] functions can be used to analyze zero-coupon bonds.

Example 1: What price should you pay for a 20-year zero-coupon bond on January 1, 1985, if you want to realize a 7 percent rate of return?

Keystrokes	Display	Comment
7 [i]	7.00	Enters desired rate of return.
0 [PMT]	0.00	Enters coupon payments.
1.011985 [ENTER]	1.011985	Enters settlement date.
1.012005	1.012005	Enters maturity date.
[f] [PRICE]	25.26	Price (as a percent of par).
10 [x]	252.57	Price in dollars.

By paying $252.57 for a 20-year, zero-coupon bond, you will obtain a realized compound yield of 7 percent.

Example 2:   A 30-year, zero-coupon bond is selling on January 1, 1985, for $95.10. What is the implicit realized compound yield you would obtain by buying the bond?

Keystrokes	Display	Comment
9.51 [PV]	9.51	Enters price (as a percent of par).
0 [PMT]	0.00	Enters coupon payments.
1.011985 [ENTER]	1.011985	Enters settlement date.
1.012015	1.012015	Enters maturity date.
[f] [YTM]	8.00	Realized compound yield.

Section
2-2
RISK MEASUREMENTS

Bonds, unlike common stocks, carry legal promises to make fixed, periodic coupon payments and to return the principal. Bond investments, thus, have no legal uncertainty regarding the cash flows that will be received. However, bond investments are not risk-free. Two main sources of risk, discussed in this section, are the volatility of interest rates and the financial ability of the company to make the future coupon and principal payments to which it is committed.

Interest rates have a significant influence in determining (1) the price of a bond (the higher the interest yields are, everything else being equal, the lower the price a bond will sell for) and (2) the average yield at which coupon payments will be reinvested (the higher the reinvestment rate is, the higher the realized compound yield). A measure that encompasses these two sources of risk is *duration.*

The financial ability of a company to make future coupon and principal payments is also important. If a firm defaulted on its bonds, the investor might not receive coupon payments and recover the original principal invested. A proxy of a company's ability to make future coupon and principal payments is the *times-interest-earned ratio* or *interest coverage ratio.*

DURATION

The concept of duration was introduced by Frederick R. Macaulay in 1938. He showed that duration is a better risk measure of the time element of a bond than term to maturity.

Duration is the present value of the weighted-average number of years that a bond takes to fully recover the principal and interest payments; that is, duration represents the present value of the average life of a bond. Duration reflects the amount and timing of expected coupon receipts and principal repayment by weighting them according to the period in which they are to be received. Duration is inversely related to coupon rates; the higher the coupon, everything else being equal, the shorter the duration, and vice versa. Duration is always shorter than term to maturity for all but zero-coupon bonds; for these bonds, duration is equal to term to maturity.

An important strategic application of the duration concept is in "immunizing" bond investments against changes in market interest rates. A bond is "immunized" when its duration equals the investor's planned holding period. In such cases, declines in bond market prices caused by rising interest rates will be totally offset by higher reinvestment rates. Similarly, increases in bond prices caused by declining interest rates will be offset by lower reinvestment rates.

The following HP-12C program makes calculating the duration of a bond very simple.* (See the formula in the Appendix.)

---

*This program assumes coupon payments are received twice a year.

KEYSTROKES	DISPLAY			KEYSTROKES	DISPLAY		
f P/R				2	22-		2
f CLEAR PRGM	00-			x	23-		20
1	01-		1	g X ≤ Y	24-	43	34
STO + 1	02-	44 40	1	g GTO 27	25-	43, 33	27
RCL 4	03-	45	4	g GTO 01	26-	43, 33	01
2	04-		2	RCL 6	27-	45	6
÷	05-		10	1	28-		1
1	06-		1	RCL 5	29-	45	4
RCL 5	07-	45	5	2	30-		2
2	08-		2	0	31-		0
0	09-		0	0	32-		0
0	10-		0	÷	33-		10
÷	11-		10	+	34-		40
+	12-		40	RCL 1	35-	45	1
RCL 1	13-	45	1	y^x	36-		21
y^x	14-		21	÷	37-		10
÷	15-		10	STO + 2	38-	44 40	2
STO + 2	16-	44 40	2	RCL 1	39-	45	1
RCL 1	17-	45	1	x	40-		20
x	18-		20	STO + 3	41-	44 40	3
STO + 3	19-	44 40	3	RCL 3	42-	45	3
RCL 1	20-	45	1	RCL 2	43-	45	2
RCL 7	21-	45	7	÷	44-		10

KEYSTROKES	DISPLAY		KEYSTROKES	DISPLAY	
2	45-	2	ENTER	54-	36
÷	46-	10	1	55-	1
R/S	47-	31	+	56-	40
RCL 5	48-	45 5	÷	57-	10
1	49-	1	x	58-	20
0	50-	0	CHS	59-	16
0	51-	0	g GTO 00	60-	43, 33 00
÷	52-	10	f P/R		
ENTER	53-	36			

REGISTERS			
n: Unused	i: Unused	PV: Unused	PMT: Unused
FV: Unused	R_0: Unused	R_1: Counter	R_2: Used
R_3: Used	R_4: Coupon payments	R_5: Yield to maturity	R_6: Redemption value
R_7: Years to maturity	R_8–$R_{.1}$: Unused		

The calculations may be made as follows:

1. Key in the program.
2. Press f CLEAR REG.
3. Key in the annual coupon payments and press STO 4.
4. Key in the yield to maturity, as a percentage, and press STO 5.
5. Key in the redemption value and press STO 6.
6. Key in the remaining number of years to maturity and press STO 7.

7. Press ⬛R/S⬛ to calculate the duration.*

8. For a new case, return to step 2.

Example: Kini Komputers, Inc., issued a bond series with the following characteristics:

Par value	$1000
Coupon rate	14% payable semiannually
Coupon payments	$70 twice a year
Term to maturity	6 years
Market price	$980
Yield to maturity	14.51%

Calculate the duration of this bond.

Keystrokes	Display	Comment
⬛f⬛ CLEAR ⬛REG⬛	0.00	Clears registers.
140 ⬛STO⬛ 4	140.00	Stores annual coupon payments.
14.51 ⬛STO⬛ 5	14.51	Stores yield to maturity.
1000 ⬛STO⬛ 6	1000.00	Stores redemption value.
6 ⬛STO⬛ 7	6.00	Stores term to maturity.
⬛R/S⬛	4.23	Duration.

INTEREST RATE RISK

The term *interest rate risk* refers to the fluctuations in a bond's price caused by changes in market interest rates. As interest rates change, the price of a bond also changes. The responsiveness of a bond's prices to a change in interest rates is

---

*This calculation may take a substantial amount of time, during which the calculator will display *running.*

known as the elasticity, E, of price with respect to interest rates.

$$E = \frac{\% \text{ change in price}}{\% \text{ change in interest rates}}$$

The price elasticity of a bond can be stated as a function of its duration, D, and the initial yield to maturity, YTM, as follows:*

$$-E = D \frac{YTM}{1 + YTM}$$

The HP-12C program used to calculate the duration of a bond can also be used to determine the price elasticity of the bond. Once the duration has been calculated, press R/S to calculate the price elasticity.

Example 1:   What is the responsiveness or elasticity of the Kini Komputers, Inc., bond price to a 1.00 percent increase in yield to maturity?

Keystrokes	Display	Comment
R/S	−0.54	Elasticity.
f 4	−0.5360	

The price of the bond would decrease 0.54 percent.

Example 2:   Because of a tight monetary policy, the required rate of return on bonds like the one Kini Komputers issued has increased from 14.51 percent to 15.60 percent. How much will the price of the bond decline?

*Since the price and yield to maturity of a bond move inversely to one another, the elasticity, E, is always negative.

Keystrokes	Display	Comment
14.51 ENTER	14.51	Enters initial *YTM*.
15.60	15.60	Enters new *YTM*.
△ %	7.51	Percentage increase in *YTM*.
.536 CHS	−0.536	Enters price elasticity.
×	−4.03	Percentage decline in price.

REFERENCES

1. M. H. Hopewell and G. G. Kaufman, "Bond Price Volatility and Term to Maturity: A Generalized Respecification," *American Economic Review*, September 1973, pp. 749–753.

2. Jack C. Francis, *Investments: Analysis and Management,* 3d ed. (McGraw-Hill Book Company, New York, 1980), pp. 203–208.

INTEREST COVERAGE RATIO

The *interest coverage ratio* is a measure of the ability of a firm to meet fixed-payment debt obligations such as coupon payments. This ratio is calculated as follows:

$$\text{Interest coverage ratio} = \frac{\text{income before interest and taxes}}{\text{debt interest payments}}$$

The higher this ratio is, the greater the firm's ability to make debt interest payments.

Example: The 1985 income statement of Kini Komputers, Inc., is as follows:

Net sales	$5750
Cost of goods sold	2384
Gross margin	3366

Operating expenses	1293
Operating income	2073
Other income	250
Income before interest and taxes	2323
Interest on bonds	850
Income before taxes	1473
Income taxes @ 45 percent	663
Net income	$ 810

What is the interest coverage ratio?

Keystrokes	Display	Comment
2323 ENTER	2323.00	Enters income before interest and taxes.
850	850.00	Enters interest payments.
÷	2.73	Interest coverage ratio.

Thus, the company's earnings were high enough to more than cover the fixed-payment debt obligations to which it was committed. As a matter of fact, earnings before interest and taxes could decline 63.4 percent and the company would still be able to make all debt payments.

Keystrokes	Display	Comment
2.73 ENTER	2.73	
1.00 △ %	−63.37	Safety margin.

This ratio should be calculated for a number of years. Trend analysis could then be used to determine in what directions it has been moving and to estimate what the ratio will be in the future.

Section
2-3
BOND
VALUATION MODEL

The value of bonds, like the value of common stock, may be calculated by discounting to the present the expected future cash flows—i.e., coupon payments and repayment of principal. Since there is very little uncertainty regarding the timing and amount of these cash flows, at least for high-quality bonds, the present-value method can be satisfactorily used.

The value or market price for a bond can be calculated using the [f] [PRICE] function.

Example 1: You are planning to buy a 12 percent coupon bond that will mature in 5 years. What price should you pay for this bond? Assume that today is October 11, 1985, and that you require a 14 percent yield to maturity or rate of return on this type of investment.

Keystrokes	Display	Comment
[f] CLEAR [FIN]	0.00	Clears financial registers.
14 [i]	14.00	Enters desired yield to maturity.
12 [PMT]	12.00	Enters coupon rate.
10.111985 [ENTER]	10.111985	Enters purchase date.
10.111990	10.111990	Enters redemption date.
[f] [PRICE]	92.98	Price (as a percentage of par).
10 [x]	929.76	Actual price.

Whenever the bond is likely to be called, the redemption date that should be used is the call date, not the maturity date. If the redemption value is higher than the par value of the bond, the $\boxed{\text{f}}$ $\boxed{\text{NPV}}$ function has to be used.

Example 2: What price should you pay for the bond described in Example 1 if you think it will be called on October 11, 1988, at a 12 percent premium?

Keystrokes	Display	Comment
$\boxed{\text{f}}$ CLEAR $\boxed{\text{FIN}}$	0.00	Clears financial registers.
0 $\boxed{\text{g}}$ $\boxed{\text{CFo}}$	0.00	Enters purchase price (to be determined).
60 $\boxed{\text{g}}$ $\boxed{\text{CFj}}$	60.00	Enters semiannual coupon payments.
5 $\boxed{\text{g}}$ $\boxed{\text{Nj}}$	5.00	Enters number of periods during which only $60 is received.
1000 $\boxed{\text{ENTER}}$ $\boxed{\text{ENTER}}$	1000.00	Enters par value.
.12 $\boxed{\times}$ $\boxed{+}$	1120.00	Call price.
60 $\boxed{+}$ $\boxed{\text{g}}$ $\boxed{\text{CFj}}$	1180.00	Enters cash flow received during last period.
14 $\boxed{\text{ENTER}}$ 2 $\boxed{\div}$ $\boxed{\text{i}}$	7.00	Enters required rate of return on a semiannual basis.
$\boxed{\text{f}}$ $\boxed{\text{NPV}}$	1032.30	Price you should pay to realize a 14% rate of return.

Section
2-4
BOND SWAPS

Active management of a bond portfolio requires in some instances that a bond be "swapped" for another. *Bond swapping* consists of selling a bond currently held and simultaneously buying a different one in its place.

Bond swaps are undertaken with a sole purpose: to improve the bond portfolio. This improvement may come through an increase in the portfolio's current income, capital appreciation potential, yield to maturity, quality, or a combination thereof. However, not all swaps end up improving the portfolio. The bond market may move in the "wrong" direction and the expected improvements may not materialize. As a matter of fact, the bond portfolio manager may incur serious losses. Thus, great care must be taken in evaluating potential swaps.

A bond swap improves the portfolio's performance when the expected yield to be realized (realized compound yield) on the purchased bond is higher than on the bond sold. By substracting the realized compound yield of the sold bond from the one on the purchased bond, we can measure by how much the portfolio improved. This difference is the value of the swap.

The value of a swap is measured in terms of basis points. A *basis point* is one hundredth of a percentage point. For example, if a bond swap increases the realized compound yield by 1.28 percent, the value of the swap is said to be 128 basis points.

Among all the bond swaps sophisticated investors use, the three most popular are:

- Substitution swap
- Market-sector spread swap
- Pure-yield pickup swap

An HP-12C program has been developed for use in analyzing the value of any of these three swaps. This program assumes that

1. All adjustments and realignments in prices and yields to maturity will take place within 1 year of the swap date, which is called the *workout period*.
2. A coupon payment date occurs the day before the swap takes place.

KEYSTROKES	DISPLAY		KEYSTROKES	DISPLAY	
f P/R			g GTO 25	22- 43, 33,	25
f CLEAR PRGM	00-		RCL 3	23- 45	3
RCL 3	01- 45	3	g GTO 26	24- 43, 33	26
i	02-	12	RCL 4	25- 45	4
RCL 2	03- 45	2	X><Y	26-	34
PMT	04-	14	R↓	27-	33
R↓	05-	33	2	28-	2
ENTER	06-	36	0	29-	0
EEX	07-	26	0	30-	0
6	08-	6	÷	31-	10
1/X	09-	22	X	32-	20
+	10-	40	RCL 2	33- 45	2
X><Y	11-	34	1	34-	1
f PRICE	12- 42	21	0	35-	0
1	13-	1	X	36-	20
0	14-	0	+	37- 40	
X	15-	20	RCL 6	38- 45	6
STO 6	16- 44	6	+	39-	40
RCL 2	17- 45	2	RCL 1	40- 45	1
5	18-	5	÷	41-	10
X	19-	20	2	42-	2
RCL 5	20- 45	5	1/X	43-	22
g X=0	21- 43	35	Yˣ	44-	21

KEYSTROKES	DISPLAY		KEYSTROKES	DISPLAY	
1	45-	1	[X><Y]	59-	34
[-]	46-	30	1	60-	1
2	47-	2	0	61-	0
[x]	48-	20	0	62-	0
[RCL] 9	49-	45 9	[x]	63-	20
[g] [X=0]	50-	43 35	[g] [GTO] 00	64-	43, 33 00
[g] [GTO] 55	51-	43, 33 55	[RCL] 8	65-	45 8
[X><Y]	52-	34	[RCL] 7	66-	45 7
[STO] 8	53-	44 8	[-]	67-	30
[g] [GTO] 60	54-	43, 33 60	[EEX]	68-	26
[X><Y]	55-	34	4	69-	4
[STO] 7	56-	44 7	[x]	70-	20
1	57-	1	[g] [GTO] 00	71-	43, 33 00
[STO] 9	58-	44 9	[f] [P/R]		

REGISTERS			
n: Unused	i: Used	PV: Used	PMT: Used
FV: Used	R_0: Unused	R_1: Purchase price	R_2: Coupon rate
R_3: YTM	R_4: Reinvestment rate	R_5: Used	R_6: New market price
R_7: Realized yield bond held	R_8: Realized yield swap candidate	R_9: Used	$R_{.0}$: Unused

The calculations may be made as follows:

1. Key in the program.
2. Press ⊤ CLEAR REG.
3. If you expect interest rates to change within the first 6 months of the workout period, key in 1 and press STO 5.
4. To calculate the expected realized compound yield of the bond currently held, do the following:
   a. Key in the initial market price and press STO 1.
   b. Key in the coupon rate and press STO 2.
   c. Key in the expected yield to maturity at the end of the workout period and press STO 3.
   d. Key in the reinvestment rate and press STO 4.
   e. Key in the maturity date (MM.DDYYYY), press ENTER, and key in the trading settlement date (MM.DDYYYY).
   f. Press R/S.
5. To calculate the expected realized compound yield of the swap candidate, repeat steps 4a through 4f.*
6. To determine the value of the swap, key in g GTO 65 and press R/S.
7. To analyze another swap candidate, go back to step 5.
8. For a new case, go back to step 2.

SUBSTITUTION SWAP

The bonds involved in this swap are equivalent in quality, coupon, and term to maturity. These bonds, however, have different yields to maturity and, hence, different prices. This imbalance is expected to be corrected during the workout period, creating an attractive capital gains opportunity. Thus, by

*Note that in some instances, bonds will differ only in their purchase price. In such cases, steps 4b through 4d need not be repeated.

switching to the underpriced bond before the yield imbalance is corrected, the bond investor will be able to obtain a higher realized compound yield.

Example 1:   Mr. Manning currently holds a 12 percent coupon, 25-year maturity bond priced at $1000 to yield 12 percent. The bond-trading settlement date is October 11, 1985. Two new bond issues with the same coupon and maturity are selling under the following terms:

A bond $992.17 to yield 12.10 percent
B bond $1007.94 to yield 11.90 percent

Assuming that Mr. Manning's reinvestment rate is 12 percent and that bonds will yield 12 percent at the end of the workout period, what can he do to improve the return on his bond portfolio?

Keystrokes	Display	Comment
f CLEAR REG	0.00	Clears registers.
1000 STO 1	1000.00	Enters market price.
12 STO 2	12.00	Enters coupon rate.
12 STO 3	12.00	Enters expected yield to maturity.
12 STO 4	12.00	Enters reinvestment rate.
10.112010 ENTER	10.112010	Enters maturity date.
10.111985	10.111985	Enters trading settlement date.
R/S	12.00	Expected realized compound yield during the 1-year workout period on the bond held.
992.17 STO 1	992.17	Enters market price of A bond.
10.112010 ENTER	10.112010	Enters maturity date.
10.111985	10.111985	Enters trading settlement date.
R/S	12.83	Expected realized compound yield on the A bond during the 1-year workout period.
g GTO 65 R/S	83.49	Value of A-bond swap in basis points.
1007.94 STO 1	1007.94	Enters market price of B bond.
10.112010 ENTER	10.112010	Enters maturity date.
10.111985	10.111985	Enters trading settlement date.
R/S	11.16	Expected realized compound yield on B bond during the 1-year workout period.
g GTO 65 R/S	−83.67	Value of B-bond swap in basis points.

Mr. Manning can improve his portfolio's return by selling the bond he currently owns and simultaneously buying the A bond. This swap will increase his return by 83.49 basis points. The B bond seems to be overvalued. If Mr. Manning bought this bond, his return would decrease by 83.67 basis points.

Example 2: What would the value of this swap be if interest rates rose over the next 6 months to 13 percent and maintained this level throughout the rest of the year?*

Keystrokes	Display	Comment
f CLEAR REG	0.00	Clears registers.
1 STO 5	1.00	Indicates that interest rates are expected to change within the first 6 months of the workout period.
1000 STO 1	1000.00	Enters market price.
12 STO 2	12.00	Enters coupon rate.
13 STO 3	13.00	Enters expected yield to maturity.
13 STO 4	13.00	Enters reinvestment rate.
10.112010 ENTER	10.112010	Enters maturity date.
10.111985	10.111985	Enters trading settlement date.
R/S	5.01	Expected realized compound yield during the 1-year workout period on the bond held.
992.17 STO 1	992.17	Enters market price of A bond.
10.112010 ENTER	10.112010	Enters maturity date.
10.111985	10.111985	Enters trading settlement date.
R/S	5.82	Expected realized compound yield on A bond during the 1-year workout period.
g GTO 65 R/S	80.74	Value of A-bond swap in basis points.

MARKET-SECTOR SPREAD SWAP

The bonds involved in this type of swap are in two different market sectors. Investors attempt to improve their bond portfolios by executing a market-sector spread swap when they

*If interest rates rise, so will the rates at which coupon payments will be reinvested and the yield at which bonds will sell.

think that the yield spreads between these bonds are temporarily out of line. If spreads are expected to narrow, an investor will generally be able to realize a gain by swapping into the bond with the higher expected yield to maturity. When the yield spread narrows, the investor will be able to realize a capital gain. If, on the other hand, spreads are expected to widen, the investor will generally realize a gain by swapping into the bond with the lower expected yield to maturity.

Example 1:   Assume that on January 1, 1985, you held a 13 percent coupon, 30-year-maturity bond selling at $1000 to yield 13 percent. You expect this bond to maintain its 13 percent yield to maturity throughout the workout period. You have the option of swapping into one of the following bonds:

A bond   30-year, 8 percent coupon selling at $738.25 to yield 11 percent

B bond   30-year, 16 percent coupon selling at $1140.39 to yield 14 percent

Your reinvestment rate will be 13 percent, and you expect the intermarket spread to widen by 30 basis points in which the yield on the A bond will fall from 11 percent to 10.7 percent and the yield on the B bond will rise from 14 percent to 14.30 percent.

Which of the possible two swaps will improve the return on your bond portfolio?

Keystrokes	Display	Comment
ⓕ CLEAR [REG]	0.00	Clears registers.
1000 [STO] 1	1000.00	Enters market price.
13 [STO] 2	13.00	Enters coupon rate.
13 [STO] 3	13.00	Enters expected yield to maturity.
13 [STO] 4	13.00	Enters reinvestment rate.
1.012015 [ENTER]	1.012015	Enters maturity date.
1.011985	1.011985	Enters trading settlement date.
[R/S]	13.00	Expected realized compound yield during the 1-year workout period on the bond held.
738.25 [STO] 1	738.25	Enters market price of A bond.
8 [STO] 2	8.00	Enters coupon rate of A bond.
10.7 [STO] 3	10.70	Enters expected yield to maturity on A bond during the 1-year workout period.
1.012015 [ENTER]	1.012015	Enters maturity date.
1.011985	1.011985	Enters trading settlement date.
[R/S]	13.66	Expected realized compound yield of A bond during the 1-year workout period.
ⓖ [GTO] 65 [R/S]	66.05	Value of A-bond swap in basis points.
1140.39 [STO] 1	1140.39	Enters market price of B bond.
16 [STO] 2	16.00	Enters coupon rate of B bond.
14.3 [STO] 3	14.30	Enters expected yield to maturity on B bond.
1.012015 [ENTER]	1.012015	Enters maturity date.
1.011985	1.011985	Enters trading settlement date.
[R/S]	12.05	Expected realized compound yield on B-bond during the 1-year workout period.
ⓖ [GTO] 65 [R/S]	−95.26	Value of B-bond swap in basis points.

Thus, if you expect the intermarket spread to widen, the A-bond swap rather than the B-bond swap will increase your bond portfolio return.

Example 2: Referring to Example 1, what swap will improve your portfolio if the intermarket spread narrows 30 basis points? The yield on the A bond will rise from 11 percent to 11.3 percent and the yield on the B bond will fall from 14 percent to 13.7 percent.*

Keystrokes	Display	Comment
738.25 [STO] 1	738.25	Enters market price of A bond.
8 [STO] 2	8.00	Enters coupon rate of A bond.
11.3 [STO] 3	11.30	Enters expected yield to maturity on A bond.
1.012015 [ENTER]	1.012015	Enters maturity date.
1.011985	1.011985	Enters trading settlement date.
[R/S]	8.53	Expected realized compound yield on A bond during the 1-year workout period.
[g] [GTO] 65 [R/S]	−446.36	Value of A-bond swap in basis points.
1140.39 [STO] 1	1140.39	Enters market price of B bond.
16 [STO] 2	16.00	Enters coupon rate of B bond.
13.7 [STO] 3	13.70	Enters expected yield to maturity on B bond.
1.012015 [ENTER]	1.012015	Enters maturity date.
1.011985	1.011985	Enters trading settlement date.
[R/S]	15.95	Expected realized compound yield on B bond during the 1-year workout period.
[g] [GTO] 65 [R/S]	294.59	Value of B-bond swap in basis points.

Now, under the assumptions of Example 2, the B-bond swap will enhance the portfolio performance, whereas the A-bond swap will not.

*It is not necessary to repeat the calculations for the bond currently held. These calculations were stored inside the calculator in Example 1.

PURE-YIELD PICKUP SWAP

The pure-yield pickup swap is a long-term swap; that is, investors plan to hold the swapped bond until maturity. In addition, this swap, in contrast to the market-sector spread swap, entails little estimation of the future market rates.

This swap involves bonds of similar quality and maturity. Investors, by swapping out of low-coupon-rate bonds with lower yields into bonds with higher coupon rates and higher yields, may realize an increase in yield to maturity and current yield.

Example: On January 1, 1985, your good friend and neighbor owns a 10-year, 12 percent coupon bond priced at $894.06, to yield 14 percent and maturing on January 1, 1995. She would like to have a higher current income and turns to you for advice on another bond she has heard about: a 10-year, 14 percent coupon bond selling at $958.91 to yield 14.8 percent. What would you recommend? Assume the reinvestment rate is 14 percent.

Keystrokes	Display	Comment
f CLEAR REG	0.00	Clears registers.
894.06 STO 1	894.06	Enters market price.
12 STO 2	12.00	Enters coupon rate.
14 STO 3	14.00	Enters expected yield to maturity.
14 STO 4	14.00	Enters reinvestment rate.
1.011995 ENTER	1.011995	Enters maturity date.
1.011985	1.011985	Enters trading settlement date.
R/S	14.00	Expected realized compound yield during the 1-year workout period on bond held.
958.91 STO 1	958.91	Enters market price of swap candidate.
14 STO 2	14.00	Enters coupon rate.
14.8 STO 3	14.80	Enters expected yield to maturity.
1.011995 ENTER	1.011995	Enters maturity date.
1.011985	1.011985	Enters trading settlement date
R/S	14.77	Expected realized compound yield on swap candidate during the 1-year workout period.
g GTO 65 R/S	77.28	Value of swap in basis points.

On the basis of a higher current income and expected realized yield, you can advise your friend to buy the bond.

REFERENCE

Sidney Homer and Martin L. Leibowitz, *Inside the Yield Book: New Tools for Bond Market Strategy* (Prentice-Hall, Englewood Cliffs, N.J., 1972), chaps. 6 and 7.

Chapter
THREE

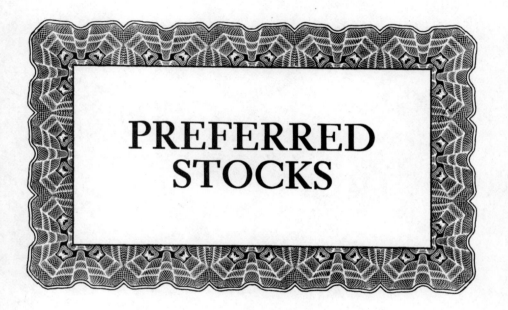

PREFERRED
STOCKS

Preferred stock is regarded as a "hybrid" security because it has features similar to both common stock and bonds.

On the one hand, preferred stock, like common stock, represents a position of ownership of a corporation. The term *preferred* refers to the preferential treatment these stocks have over common stock regarding the liquidation of assets and the distribution of income.

On the other hand, preferred stock receives payments that are stipulated as a fixed percentage of its par value, just as bond coupons do. However, unlike bond coupon payments, preferred stock dividends are perpetual. Unless the preferred stock is called or converted, preferred stockholders will receive dividend payments as long as the company continues to exist (and to show profits).

Although preferred stock is part of a corporation's equity, investors regard it, for valuation purposes only, as a bond variant. Thus, bond valuation principles can be used in determining the yield and value of preferred stock.

Section
3-1
RETURN
MEASUREMENTS

NOMINAL YIELD

The nominal yield is the stated dividend yield as a percentage of part value. For example, the nominal dividend yield of a $50 par value preferred stock paying annual dividends of $6 is 12 percent, as shown below.

Keystrokes	Display	Comment
6 ENTER	6.00	Enters annual dividends.
50	50.00	Enters par value.
÷	0.12	Nominal yield.
100 x	12.00	Nominal yield (%).

CURRENT YIELD

The current yield is calculated by dividing the annual dividend payments by the stock's current market price. If, for example, the previous preferred stock were selling for $46, the current yield would be 13.04 percent, as shown below.

Keystrokes	Display	Comment
6 ENTER	6.00	Enters annual dividends.
46	46.00	Enters market price.
÷	0.13	Current yield.
100 x	13.04	Current yield (%).

Section
3-2
RISK
MEASUREMENT

Because a preferred stock cannot be regarded entirely as either a common stock or a bond, some conceptual problems arise when applying modern risk measures such as beta and duration, which are used with common stocks and bonds. Thus, traditional risk evaluation approaches are used.

In evaluating preferred stock, a question immediately arises about the ability of the issuing corporation to service the fixed dividend payments to which it is committed. By analyzing the issuer's future earnings potential and fixed financial charges, one can evaluate the likelihood that preferred dividends will be paid. The more likely it is that the future dividends will be paid, the less risky (uncertain) the investment will be.

The ability of the issuing company to make future dividend payments is measured by the *total financial-charge coverage ratio:*

$$\text{Financial-charge coverage ratio} = \frac{\text{income before financial charges and corporate taxes}}{\text{debt interest} + \dfrac{\text{preferred dividends}}{(1 + \text{tax rate})}}$$

Since preferred stock dividend payments are not deductible for corporate tax purposes, they have to be restated on a before-tax basis to make them comparable to debt interest payments. To determine the ability of the company to pay future preferred dividends, this ratio should be projected as far into the future as reasonable estimates permit.

Example: International Investments' income statement for 1985 is as follows:

Net sales	$36,217
Cost of goods sold	18,335
Gross margin	17,882
Operating expenses	9,846
Operating income	8,036
Other income	3,452
Income before interest and taxes	11,488
Interest on bonds	1,968
Income before taxes	9,520
Income taxes @ 42%	3,998
Net income	5,522
Preferred dividends	2,017

Keystrokes	Display	Comment
2017 ENTER	2017.00	Enters preferred dividends.
1 ENTER .42 −	0.58	One minus corporate tax rate.
÷	3477.59	Preferred dividends on a before-tax basis.
1968 +	5455.59	Total financial charges.
11488 x> <y ÷	2.11	Total financial charges coverage ratio.

Section
3-3
VALUATION MODEL

The value of preferred stock may be calculated by using the present-value model. As discussed in the previous sections, the present-value model discounts at a derived rate of return all future expected cash receipts. If preferred stock dividends are expected to be perpetual, we need to discount an infinite stream of future receipts.

The present value of an infinite stream of constant receipts is given by the equation

$$\text{Present value} = \frac{\text{annual dividend payments}}{\text{discount rate}}$$

Example 1: You are considering investing in the preferred stock of International Investments, Inc. The stock pays a $14 annual dividend and has no call features. How much will you be willing to pay for 1 share if your required rate of return is 16 percent?

Keystrokes	Display	Comment
14 [ENTER]	14.00	Enters annual dividend.
.16	0.16	Enters required rate of return.
[÷]	87.50	Price at which you will earn a 16 percent return.

Given the current market price and annual dividend payments of the preferred stock, the discount rate at which the market

capitalizes the stream of future dividends can be calculated by
using the equation

$$\text{Market discount rate} = \frac{\text{annual dividends}}{\text{current market price}}$$

If the stock were bought at the current market price, the rate of
return the buyer would earn would equal the market discount
rate.

Example 2: International Investments' preferred stock is
currently selling for $97.40. What is the implicit market
discount rate?

Keystrokes	Display	Comment
14 ENTER	14.00	Enters annual dividend.
97.4	97.40	Enters current market price.
÷	0.14	Market discount rate.

In case the preferred stock issue contains some call or
conversion features, the investment horizon should extend only
to the conversion or call date. To determine the value of a
convertible or callable preferred stock, see the convertible
securities and bond valuation models discussed in Chapter 4,
Section 4-2, and Chapter 2, Section 2-1, respectively.

Chapter
FOUR

WARRANTS AND CONVERTIBLE SECURITIES

Section
4-1
WARRANTS

A *warrant* is an option which permits its owner to purchase a designated number of shares of common stock at a predetermined price within a specified time period. Warrants are issued by corporations and are usually attached to bonds or preferred stocks as a sweetener. For example, if a corporation issues a new bond or preferred stock, the attachment of warrants may enhance their marketability, while lowering the required interest or preferred dividend rate.

Each warrant contains two important provisions: (1) the exercise price, or the price at which common shares can be purchased, and (2) the expiration date of the warrant, i.e., the last date on which the warrant can be exercised. Most warrants are issued on a long-term basis, and a few have perpetual lives. If the option to purchase the common stock with the warrant is not exercised within the specified time period, the warrant becomes worthless on the expiration date.

Warrants are usually detachable and are actively traded on organized exchanges as well as in the over-the-counter market.

Warrants have a market value as well as a theoretical value. The market value of a warrant is the price that is quoted in the market.

THEORETICAL VALUE

The theoretical value of a warrant, TV_w, is a function of the current market price of the common stock, MP_c, the exercise price of the warrant, EP_w, and the number of shares that can be bought with one warrant, N.

$$TV_w = (MP_c - EP_w)N$$

Example: Mangalore Ores, Inc., has issued warrants. Each warrant entitles its owner to purchase 3 shares of common stock at $24 per share. The current market price of the stock is $26. What is the theoretical value of these warrants?

Keystrokes	Display	Comment
26 ENTER	26.00	Enters MP_c.
24	24.00	Enters EP_w.
─	2.00	
3	3.00	Enters N.
×	6.00	TV_w.

The theoretical value represents the minimum price for which a warrant will sell. Frequently, the exercise price is greater than the current market price of the stock. In such cases, the theoretical value of a warrant is negative. However, since a negative value is meaningless, the theoretical value is considered to be zero.

PREMIUM

A warrant's premium is the excess of its current market price, MP_w, over its theoretical value. The premium amount depends on the potential for the common stock to rise in the future and on the period remaining during which the warrant can be exercised.

The premium is sometimes calculated as follows:

$$\text{Premium } (\%) = \left[\frac{(MP_w/N) + EP_w}{MP_c} - 1 \right] 100$$

This percentage premium reveals how much the common stock has to appreciate before the theoretical value exceeds the market price of the warrant.

Example: If Mangalore Ores' warrants are selling for $8, how much does the price of the common stock have to increase for the investor to break even?

Keystrokes	Display	Comment
8 ENTER	8.00	Enters MP_w.
3	3.00	Enters N.
÷	2.67	Premium per share.
24	24.00	Enters EP_w.
+	26.67	Total cost per share.
26	26.00	Enters MP_c.
X><Y Δ%	2.56	Percentage increase in common stock price necessary in order to break even, if the warrant is exercised.

Section
4-2
CONVERTIBLE SECURITIES

Convertible securities are bonds and preferred stocks that can, at the owner's option, be converted into other types of securities in accordance with specific terms set forth in the contract. Usually, convertible securities are convertible into common stock.

The unique feature of convertible securities is that they possess the advantages of more conservative senior securities that guarantee fixed interest or dividend payments. In addition, convertible securities participate in the growth and appreciation potential of the underlying securities through their conversion rights.

Because of the conversion privilege, the yield on convertible securities is normally lower than the yield on nonconvertibles of similar quality and maturity.

The ratios, prices, and values described below are frequently used in evaluating convertible securities.

CONVERSION RATIO

The *conversion ratio* is the number of shares of common or preferred stock into which each bond is convertible.

CONVERSION PARITY PRICE

The *conversion parity price* is the actual cost a holder of a convertible security will pay for the common stock if the bond is converted. To calculate the conversion parity price, divide the price paid for the convertible security by the conversion ratio. (See the formula in the Appendix.)

INVESTMENT VALUE

The *investment value,* or straight bond value, of a convertible security is the market value the security would have without any conversion features. The investment value is a support level below which the price of a convertible bond will not decline. (See the formula in the Appendix.)

CONVERSION VALUE

The *conversion value,* or stock value, of a convertible security is the value the bond would have if it were converted into stock immediately. This value can be derived by multiplying the conversion rate by the current stock price. The conversion value provides an additional support level for the price of the bond. Whenever the investment value is higher than the conversion value, the investment value will be the actual support level. By the same token, whenever the conversion value is higher than the investment value, the conversion value will be the actual support level. (See the formula in the Appendix.)

PREMIUM OVER INVESTMENT VALUE

The *premium over investment value* is a measure of how much the investment value of the convertible security has to go up before it reaches its current market price. (See the formula in the Appendix.)

PREMIUM OVER CONVERSION VALUE

The *premium over conversion value,* which is very similar to the premium over investment value, is a measure of how much the conversion value has to go up before it reaches the current market price. (See the formula in the Appendix.)

These values can be represented as follows:

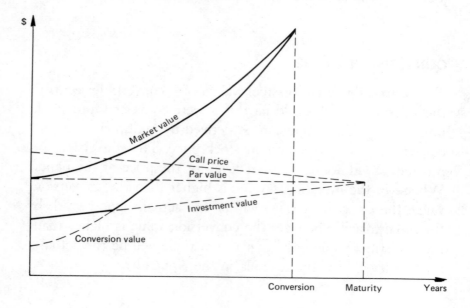

VALUATION MODEL

The theoretical value of a convertible security at a given time is equal to the present value of (1) the future dividend or interest payments and (2) the expected conversion value at the conversion date. These future flows are discounted at the investor's required rate of return. Alternatively, by finding the discount rate that makes the present market price of the bond equal to the future cash flows, one can determine the market's required rate of return on these investments. (See the formula in the Appendix.)

The conversion value at the conversion date is equal to the conversion rate times the expected market price of the common stock. The future market price can be approximated by assuming that the current market price will increase at a certain average annual rate.

The following HP-12C program has been designed to facilitate the analysis of convertible securities.

KEYSTROKES	DISPLAY		KEYSTROKES	DISPLAY	
f P/R			ENTER	21-	36
f CLEAR PRGM	00-		RCL 2	22-	45 2
RCL 1	01-	45 1	−	23-	30
RCL 9	02-	45 9	RCL 2	24-	45 2
÷	03-	10	X> <Y	25-	34
R/S	04-	31	% T	26-	23
PMT	05-	14	R/S	27-	31
R ↓	06-	33	R ↓	28-	33
i	07-	12	R ↓	29-	33
R ↓	08-	33	RCL 3	30-	45 3
f PRICE	09-	42 21	−	31-	30
1	10-	1	RCL 3	32-	45 3
0	11-	0	X> <Y	33-	34
X	12-	20	% T	34-	23
STO 2	13-	44 2	R/S	35-	31
R/S	14-	31	g CFo	36-	43 13
RCL 6	15-	45 6	RCL 7	37-	45 7
RCL 9	16-	49 9	5	38-	5
X	17-	20	X	39-	20
STO 3	18-	44 3	g CFj	40-	43 14
R/S	19-	31	RCL 4	41-	45 4
ENTER	20-	36	2	42-	2

KEYSTROKES	DISPLAY		KEYSTROKES	DISPLAY		
☒	43-	20	5	61-		5
1	44-	1	☒	62-		20
☐ −	45-	30	☐ +	63-		40
☐ g ☐ Nj	46-	43 15	☐ g ☐ CFj	64-	43	14
RCL 6	47-	45 6	RCL 0	65-	45	0
1	48-	1	☐ g ☐ X=0	66-	43	35
RCL 8	49-	45 8	☐ g ☐ GTO 72	67-	43, 33	72
1	50-	1	☐ f ☐ IRR	68-	42	15
0	51-	0	2	69-		2
0	52-	0	☒	70-		20
☐ ÷	53-	10	☐ g ☐ GTO 00	71-	43, 33	00
☐ +	54-	40	RCL 5	72-	45	5
RCL 4	55-	45 4	2	73-		2
☐ Yˣ	56-	21	☐ ÷	74-		10
☒	57-	20	☐ i	75-		12
RCL 9	58-	45 9	☐ f ☐ NPV	76-	42	13
☒	59-	20	☐ g ☐ GTO 00	77-	43, 33	00
RCL 7	60-	45 7	☐ f ☐ P/R			

REGISTERS*			
n: Used	i: Used	PV: Used	PMT: Used
FV: Unused	R_0: Used	R_1: Bond market price	R_2: Investment
R_3: Conversion value	R_4: Years to conversion	R_5: Discount rate	R_6: Market price of stock
R_7: Coupon rate convertible bond	R_8: Dividend growth rate	R_9: Conversion ratio	

*The initial content of registers R_1 and R_2 is as indicated. However, these registers are used during the running of the program for other purposes.

The calculations may be made as follows:

1. Key in the program.
2. Press ⌈f⌉ CLEAR ⌈REG⌉.
3. Key in purchase or market price of the convertible bond and press ⌈STO⌉ 1.
4. Key in the number of years left to conversion and press ⌈STO⌉ 4.
5. Key in your required rate of return (as a percentage) and press ⌈STO⌉ 5.
6. Key in the current market price of the stock and press ⌈STO⌉ 6.
7. Key in the coupon rate of the convertible security and press ⌈STO⌉ 7.
8. Key in the expected annual growth rate of the stock's price and press ⌈STO⌉ 8.
9. Enter the conversion ratio and press ⌈STO⌉ 9.
10. Press ⌈R/S⌉ to compute the conversion parity price.
11. Key in the purchase date (MM.DDYYYY) and press ⌈ENTER⌉.
12. Key in the maturity date (MM.DDYYYY) and press ⌈ENTER⌉.
13. Key in, as a percentage, the yield to maturity of equivalent bonds which do not have conversion options.

14. Press $\boxed{\text{RCL}}$ 7 $\boxed{\text{R/S}}$ to obtain the investment value.

15. Press $\boxed{\text{R/S}}$ to obtain the conversion value.

16. Key in the bond's purchase or current market price.

17. Press $\boxed{\text{R/S}}$ to obtain the percentage premium over investment value.

18. Press $\boxed{\text{R/S}}$ to calculate the percentage premium over conversion value.

19. Key in zero (0) and press $\boxed{\text{R/S}}$ to compute the theoretical value of the convertible security.

20. Key in the current market value of the convertible and press $\boxed{\text{CHS}}$ $\boxed{\text{g}}$ $\boxed{\text{GTO}}$ 36 $\boxed{\text{R/S}}$ to derive the actual rate of return or yield.

21. For a new case, go back to step 2.

Example 1:   On September 26, 1985, DuPonoco issued the following 25-year convertible bond:

Par value	$1000
Coupon rate	11% payable semiannually
Maturity	September 26, 2010
Market value	$1180

The conversion features were as follows:

Conversion ratio	Each bond convertible into 40 shares of common stock
Conversion date	After September 26, 1995

On September 26, 1985, the market price of the underlying common stock was $21 a share and the yield to maturity of bonds with similar quality and maturity but without conversion options was 13 percent. If, at that time, you required a 15 percent rate of return on your investments and assumed that the price of the common stock would grow at an annual rate of 8 percent, what is the price you would have been willing to pay for this convertible bond? What were the conversion parity price, investment and conversion values, and the premiums over investment value and over conversion value at the date of issue?*

Keystrokes	Display	Comment
f CLEAR REG	0.00	Clears registers.
1180 STO 1	1180.00	Stores purchase price.
10 STO 4	10.00	Stores years to conversion.
15 STO 5	15.00	Stores your required rate of return.
21 STO 6	21.00	Stores current market value of common stock.
11 STO 7	11.00	Stores coupon rate.
8 STO 8	8.00	Stores stock price's annual growth rate.
40 STO 9	40.00	Stores conversion ratio.
R/S	29.50	Conversion parity price.
9.261985 ENTER	9.261985	Enters purchase date.
9.262010 ENTER	9.262010	Enters maturity date.
13	13.00	Enters yield to maturity of equivalent straight bonds.
RCL 7 R/S	852.75	Investment value.
R/S	840.00	Conversion value.
1180	1180.00	Enters market price of convertible bond.
R/S	38.38	Premium (%) over investment value.
R/S	40.48	Premium (%) over conversion value.
0	0.00	
R/S	987.62	Theoretical value ($).

*Note that in this example you have to analyze the convertible bond as if today were September 26, 1985.

Example 2: What rate of return would you obtain if you had bought the bond on September 26, 1985, at its then-current market price?

To calculate the rate of return you would have obtained had you bought the security at $1.180, proceed as follows:

Keystrokes	Display	Comment
1180 [CHS] [g] [GTO] 36	−1180.00	
[R/S]	12.21	Rate of return.

Example 3: Five years after DuPonoco issued the convertible bonds, a friend recommends that you buy the bond. The current market price of the bond is $1250, and the common stock is selling for $29. You still require a 15 percent rate of return on your investment and still expect the stock to appreciate at an 8 percent annual rate. What should you do?

Keystrokes	Display	Comment
⨍ CLEAR REG	0.00	Clears registers.
1250 STO 1	1250.00	Stores purchase price.
5 STO 4	5.00	Stores years to conversion.
15 STO 5	15.00	Stores your required rate of return.
29 STO 6	29.00	Stores current market price of common stock.
11 STO 7	11.00	Stores coupon rate.
8 STO 8	8.00	Stores stock price's annual growth rate.
40 STO 9	40.00	Stores conversion ratio.
R/S	31.25	Conversion parity price.
9.261990 ENTER	9.261990	Enters purchase date.
9.262010 ENTER	9.262010	Enters maturity date.
13	13.00	Enters yield to maturity of equivalent straight bonds.
RCL 7 R/S	858.54	Investment value.
R/S	1160.00	Conversion value.
1250	1250.00	Enters market price of convertible bond.
R/S	45.60	Premium (%) over investment value.
R/S	7.76	Premium (%) over conversion value.
0		
R/S	1204.50	Theoretical value ($).

Since the estimated theoretical value is smaller than the current market price, you can conclude that the bond is overpriced. Thus, you should not buy this bond. If you did, your rate of return would be less than 15 percent, as shown below.

Keystrokes	Display	Comment
1250 CHS g GTO 36	−1250.00	Purchase price.
R/S	14.60	Rate of return.

Chapter
FIVE

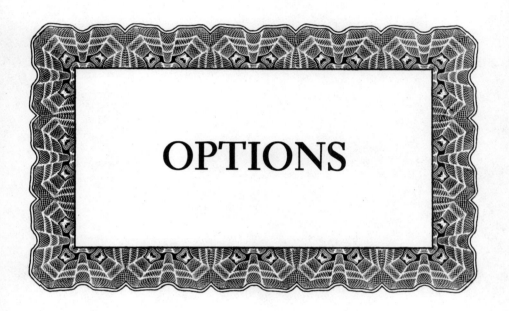

OPTIONS

An *option* is a contract in which the holder is granted the privilege to buy or sell a security at a specified price (the exercise or striking price) within a specified period of time, usually less than a year. Most options expire after 30 to 90 days. Unless otherwise noted, options are written for units of 100 shares. There are two major types of options. *Call options* give the holder the right to buy 100 shares of the optioned stock at a specified exercise price within the specified period. The option buyer is entitled to pay that price regardless of the prevailing market price at the time the privilege is exercised. *Put options* give the holder the right to sell 100 shares of the optioned stock at an exercise price specified in the contract within the predetermined period. The price paid for a call or put is also known as the *premium.*

Other options combine calls and puts in various ways. For example, a *straddle* is a combination option consisting of one call and one put. The specified exercise prices and periods of time are the same for the call and put features, and the option seller receives a single premium. A *strap* is a combination of two calls and one put, and a *strip* is a combination of two puts and one call. Call and put options have been available to investors on the over-the-counter market for a number of years, but became widely accepted and used by investors only with the founding of the Chicago Board Options Exchange in 1973.

Section
5-1
CALL OPTIONS

The profit and loss potentials of a call buyer can be depicted as follows.

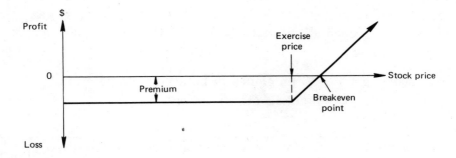

The buyer stands to lose the premium paid if the stock sells below the exercise price. However, if the price goes above the breakeven point (the exercise price plus the premium), the profits will increase point for point as the price of the stock goes up.

The profit and loss potentials of a call writer (the seller) are exactly the opposite of the buyer's profit and loss potentials, as shown below.

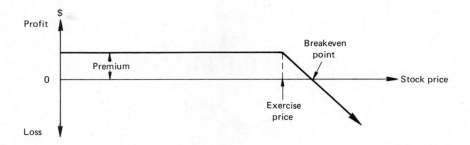

The seller's profit potential is limited by the premium received. The loss potential, however, is unlimited. The higher the stock price goes above the breakeven point, the greater the losses the option's writer will suffer. To limit this loss potential, most sellers write "covered" call options; that is, they write calls on stocks they own.

The following HP-12C program can be utilized to determine the profit and loss potentials of call options.

KEYSTROKES	DISPLAY	KEYSTROKES	DISPLAY
f P/R		X> <Y	08- 34
f CLEAR PRGM	00-	g GTO 00	09- 43, 33 00
RCL 3	01- 45 3	RCL 1	10- 45 1
–	02- 30	RCL 2	11- 45 2
RCL 2	03- 45 2	CHS	12- 16
g X ≤ Y	04- 43 34	+	13- 40
g GTO 08	05- 43, 33 08	STO 3	14- 44 3
RCL 2	06- 45 2	g GTO 00	15- 43, 33 00
g GTO 00	07- 43, 33 00	f P/R	

REGISTERS			
n: Unused	i: Unused	PV: Unused	PMT: Unused
FV: Unused	R_0: Unused	R_1: Exercise price	R_2: Premium
R_3: Breakeven point	R_4–R_8: Unused		

The calculations may be made as follows:

1. Key in the program.
2. Press ⨍ CLEAR [REG].
3. Key in the exercise price and press [STO] 1.
4. Key in the call premium and press [CHS] [STO] 2.
5. To calculate the breakeven point, press [g] [GTO] 10 [R/S].
6. To determine the profit or loss associated with a stock price, enter the price and
   a. Press [R/S] if you are buying a call.
   b. Press [R/S] [CHS] if you are writing a call.*
7. To analyze the profit or loss of a call option for different prices, go back to step 6.
8. To analyze different call options, go back to step 2.

Example 1:   You are considering buying a call option on Green Grass Gardens common stock. The call option premium is $2 per share, and the exercise price is $22. What is the breakeven price? Disregarding transaction costs, what will your profit (or loss) be if, by the expiration date, the stock sells for $18, $20, $24, $30, and $31?

*The breakeven point has to be calculated to determine the profit or loss associated with a particular call option.

Keystrokes	Display	Comment
f CLEAR REG	0.00	Clears registers
22 STO 1	22.00	Enters exercise price.
2 CHS STO 2	−2.00	Enters call premium.
g GTO 10 R/S	24.00	Breakeven point.
18 R/S	−2.00	Loss at $18.
20 R/S	−2.00	Loss at $20.
24 R/S	0.00	Profit at $24.
30 R/S	6.00	Profit at $30.
31 R/S	7.00	Profit at $31.

Example 2:   You doubt that the Green Grass Gardens common stock price will move upward during the option. You thus decide to write a call option. Disregarding transaction costs, what will your profit (or loss) be at $18, $20, $24, $26, $30, and $31?

Keystrokes	Display	Comment
$18 R/S CHS	2.00	Profit at $18.
$20 R/S CHS	2.00	Profit at $20.
$24 R/S CHS	0.00	Profit at $24.
$30 R/S CHS	−6.00	Loss at $30.
$31 R/S CHS	−7.00	Loss at $31.

Section

5-2

PUT OPTIONS

The buyer of a put option is in a situation similar to that of the buyer of a call option: the potential losses are limited to the premium paid. The buyer of a put option, however, tends to participate point for point in the stock's movements when the stock price goes below the breakeven point (the exercise price minus the premium) but not above it.

The profit and loss potentials of a put buyer are as shown below.

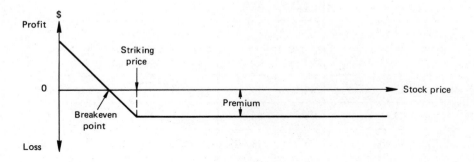

The writer of a put option, on the other hand, is in a situation similar to that of the writer of a call option: the profit potential is limited to the premium received. In the case of a put option, however, the writer of the option will make money only when the stock's price is above the breakeven point (the exercise price minus the premium). The put writer will lose money whenever the stock price falls below the breakeven point (and the put buyer exercises the option).

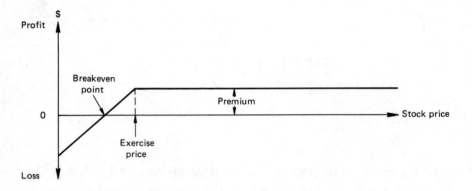

The following HP-12C program may be used in analyzing put options.

KEYSTROKES	DISPLAY	KEYSTROKES	DISPLAY
f P/R		X><Y	08- 34
f CLEAR PRGM	00-	g GTO 00	09- 43, 33 00
RCL 3	01- 45 3	RCL 1	10- 45 1
X><Y	02- 34	RCL 2	11- 45 2
−	03- 30	+	12- 40
RCL 2	04- 45 2	STO 3	13- 44 3
g X≤Y	05- 43 34	g GTO 00	14- 43, 33 00
g GTO 08	06- 43, 33 08	f P/R	
g GTO 00	07- 43, 33 00		

REGISTERS			
n: Unused	i: Unused	PV: Unused	PMT: Unused
FV: Unused	R_0: Unused	R_1: Exercise price	R_2: Premium
R_3: Breakeven point	R_4–$R_{.8}$: Unused		

The calculations may be made as follows:

1. Key in the program.
2. Press ⨍ CLEAR REG .
3. Key in the exercise price and press STO 1.
4. Key in the premium and press CHS STO 2.
5. To calculate the breakeven point, press g GTO 10 R/S .
6. To determine the profit or loss associated with a stock price, enter the price and

   a. Press R/S if you are buying a put.
   b. Press R/S CHS if you are writing a put.*
7. To analyze the profit or loss of a put option for different prices, go back to step 6.
8. To analyze different put options, go back to step 2.

Example 1:   Red Carpet Services put options are selling for $1.50 per share. The exercise price is $16¾. What are the profit and loss potentials for a put buyer if, by the option's expiration date, the stock sells at $9, $11, $14, $16, and $17? What is the breakeven point?

Keystrokes	Display	Comment
3 ENTER 4 ÷ 16 + STO 1	16.75	Enters exercise price.
1.50 CHS STO 2	−1.50	Enters put premium.
g GTO 10 R/S	15.25	Breakeven point.
9 R/S	6.25	Profit at $9.
11 R/S	4.25	Profit at $11.
14 R/S	1.25	Profit at $14.
16 R/S	−0.75	Loss at $16.
17 R/S	−1.50	Loss at $17.

*The breakeven point has to be calculated to determine the profit or loss associated with a particular call option.

Example 2:   What are the profit and loss potentials for a put writer at stock prices of $14, $17, $18, and $21?

Keystrokes	Display	Comment
g GTO 10 R/S	15.25	Breakeven point.
14 R/S CHS	−1.25	Loss at $14.
17 R/S CHS	1.50	Profit at $17.
18 R/S CHS	1.50	Profit at $18.
21 R/S CHS	1.50	Profit at $21.

REFERENCE

Donald E. Fischer and Ronald J. Jordan, *Security Analysis and Portfolio Management,* 2d ed. (Prentice-Hall, Englewood Cliffs, N.J., 1979), pp. 342–364.

Chapter
SIX

PORTFOLIO MANAGEMENT

Investors have always been concerned about measuring the investment performance of their portfolios. Before modern portfolio theory was developed, most portfolio managers tended to measure portfolio performance on the basis of a simple rate of return, usually comparing the portfolio's return with some broad yardstick, such as the Dow Jones Industrial Stock Average or another stock market index. Although investors were aware of risk, no attempt was made to measure portfolio returns in conjunction with risk. Developments in portfolio theory in the 1960s enabled investors to quantify risk and to make direct comparisons between the rates of return of alternative portfolios with different risk levels.

Analysis of a portfolio's performance entails predicting returns on the basis of risk relationships and comparing them with the returns actually earned. Models that use risk-return relationships to predict the return of individual assets and portfolios are presented in Sections 6-1 to 6-3. Section 6-4 shows how HP-12C programs can be used to evaluate the performance of investment portfolios.

Section
6-1
CHARACTERISTIC
LINE

The *characteristic line* (CL) depicts the relation between the rate of return of a security and the rate of return of the market. Thus, the CL describes a security's return in relation to the market or, in other words, the asset's systematic risk.

The CL is simply a regression line. The slope of this line is the beta of the security, and the vertical intercept is the alpha coefficient.

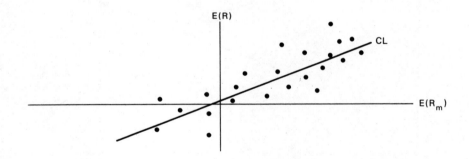

An HP-12C program to calculate a stock's beta and alpha coefficients is presented in Chapter 1, Section 1-2.

Section

6-2

SECURITY
MARKET LINE

The *security market line* (SML) was developed by J. Treynor. The SML—or the capital asset pricing model (CAPM), as it is also known—depicts the risk-return relationships for securities. Since the relevant risk measure for securities is their systematic risk (or beta), the expected return should be related to it. The SML represents these relationships as follows:

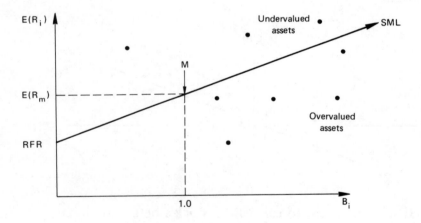

The relationship between a security's beta (B_i) and the expected return, $E(R_i)$, can be expressed as

$$E(R_i) = RFR + B_i[E(R_m)-RFR]$$

where $E(R_i)$ = expected return for an individual asset
B_i = beta of an asset

$$E(R_m) = \text{expected return for the market}$$
$$RFR = \text{risk-free rate}$$

Example: Under equilibrium conditions, what return can be expected for a security with a beta of 1.20? Assume that the expected return for the market is 14 percent and the risk-free rate is 5 percent.

Keystrokes	Display	Comment
1.20 [ENTER]	1.20	Enters beta.
14 [ENTER]	14.00	Enters the expected return for the market.
5	5.00	Enters the risk-free rate.
[−]	9.00	Risk premium return of market.
[×]	10.80	
5 [+]	15.80	Expected return for the security.

In equilibrium, all securities should plot along the SML according to their systematic risk. Securities that plot above the SML have a return higher than that implied by their level of systematic risk. These securities are considered to be undervalued. Those that plot below the SML have a return too low for their systematic risk. These securities are thus regarded as overvalued.

Although the SML was originally developed as a model for pricing capital assets like securities, its use has been extended also to portfolios. Thus, the risk-return relations of both securities and portfolios of securities can be evaluated using the SML.

Section
6-3
CAPITAL
MARKET LINE

The *capital market line* (CML) was developed by William Sharpe based on the work of Harry Markowitz. The CML depicts the risk-return relationships that prevail in the capital markets, under equilibrium conditions, for efficient portfolios.

In equilibrium, the relationship between risk and return for efficient portfolios is linear, as shown below.

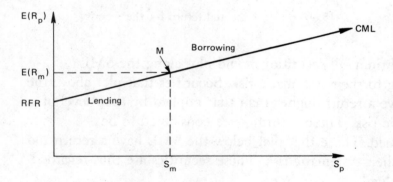

This relationship between risk and return can be represented mathematically as

$$E(R_p) = RFR + \left[\frac{E(R_m) - RFR}{S_m}\right]S_p$$

where $E(R_p)$ = expected return for a portfolio of assets
RFR = risk-free rate
$E(R_m)$ = expected return for the market portfolio
S_m = standard deviation of the market portfolio
S_p = standard deviation of a portfolio
M = market portfolio

Example: The standard deviation of a well-diversified portfolio is 11 percent. The risk-free rate is 5 percent and the expected return and risk of the market portfolio are 14 percent and 10 percent, respectively. What is the expected return for the portfolio?

Keystrokes	Display	Comment
5 ENTER	5.00	Enters risk-free rate.
14 ENTER	14.00	Enters expected return of market portfolio.
5	5.00	Enters risk-free rate.
−	9.00	Risk premium return of market.
10	10.00	Enters standard deviation of market.
÷	0.90	
11	11.00	Enters standard deviation of portfolio.
× +	14.90	Expected return of portfolio.

Sharpe argued that since the market portfolio contains all risky assets, it is a perfectly diversified portfolio. Thus, all investors would want to acquire it. Some investors would lend part of their capital at the RFR and invest the rest in the market portfolio, whereas others would borrow capital at the RFR and invest it in the market portfolio.

The rate of return which investors would obtain from this portfolio is given by

$$E(R_p) = XE(R_m) - (X-1)RFR$$

where X is the proportion of the investor's equity invested in the market portfolio. For example, if an investor borrows 25 percent to invest in the portfolio, X is equal to 1.25, and if the investor lends 20 percent, X is equal to 0.80.

The risk associated with such investments is

$$S_p = XS_m$$

Example: Assuming that the expected return and risk for the market portfolio are 15 percent and 7 percent, respectively, and that investors can lend or borrow at the *RFR* of 6 percent, what is the expected return on the "leveraged" portfolio for an investor who borrows 20 percent? On the "lending" portfolio for one who lends 15 percent? What is the risk of their portfolios?

Keystrokes	Display	Comment
1.20 ENTER	1.20	Enters proportion invested in the portfolio.
15	15.00	Enters expected return for market portfolio.
x	18.00	Gross return.
1.20 ENTER	1.20	
1 −	0.20	
6	6.00	Enters risk-free rate.
x	1.20	
−	16.80	Expected return for borrower.
1.20 ENTER	1.20	
7	7.00	Enters expected risk of market portfolio.
x	8.40	Expected risk for borrower.
.85 ENTER	0.85	Enters proportion invested in portfolio.
15	15.00	Enters expected return for market portfolio.
x	12.75	Gross return.
.85 ENTER	0.85	
1 −	−0.15	
6	6.00	Enters risk-free rate.
x	−0.90	
−	13.65	Expected return for lender.
.85 ENTER	0.85	
7	7.00	Enters expected risk of market portfolio.
x	5.95	Expected risk for lender.

Section
6-4
PERFORMANCE
EVALUATION

The purpose of evaluating the performance of a portfolio of securities is to ascertain (1) whether the return obtained was the one warranted by the level of risk assumed and (2) whether the portfolio was well diversified, i.e., whether unsystematic risk was limited.

The capital asset pricing model provides the framework within which the performance of a portfolio can be evaluated. The three most frequently used measures of performance are

- Treynor measure
- Jensen measure
- Sharpe measure

TREYNOR MEASURE

The *Treynor performance measure,* also known as the *reward-to-volatility ratio,* is based on the security market line (SML). This measure relates the portfolio's excess return to the level of systematic risk. The Treynor ratio, *T,* is defined as follows:

$$T = \frac{\text{rate of return for the portfolio} - \text{risk-free rate}}{\text{beta of the portfolio}}$$

The higher this ratio is, the greater the return obtained for the level of systematic risk assumed.

JENSEN MEASURE

The *Jensen measure* of portfolio performance is also based on the security market line. According to the SML, the return for a security or portfolio is given by the equation

$$E(R)^* = RFR + B[E(R_m)-RFR]$$

The difference between the realized return, $\overline{R}$, and the predicted return, $E(R)^*$, is known as the risk-adjusted excess return or alpha, A_p, and is described by the equation

$$A_p = \overline{R} - E(R)^*$$

Given this equation, Jensen indicated that the alpha coefficient, A_p, is a measure of the portfolio's ability to obtain above- or below-average returns. If the portfolio can consistently outperform the market, alpha will be positive; if, on the other hand, the portfolio cannot obtain a return appropriate for the portfolio's risk class, alpha will be negative; and if the capital markets are perfectly efficient, alpha will be zero.

SHARPE MEASURE

The *Sharpe composite measure* of portfolio performance is based on the capital market line (CML). Sharpe's measure, also known as the *reward-to-variability ratio,* relates a portfolio's excess return to its total risk as measured by the standard deviation.

$$S = \frac{\text{rate of return for the portfolio}) - \text{risk-free rate}}{\text{standard deviation of the portfolio}}$$

The risk-adjusted excess return (or alpha) of a portfolio can also be calculated by using the CML. According to the CML, the predicted return, $E(R)^*$, of a portfolio is

$$E(R)^* = RFR + \left[\frac{E(R_m) - RFR}{S_m}\right] S_p$$

The following HP-12C program can be used to calculate the Treyner and Sharpe ratios and the overall excess returns based on either the SML (Jensen's alpha) or the CML.

KEYSTROKES	DISPLAY	KEYSTROKES	DISPLAY
f P/R		X	21- 20
f CLEAR PRGM	00-	RCL 1	22- 45 1
STO 4	01- 44 4	+	23- 40
R↓	02- 33	R/S	24- 31
STO 5	03- 44 5	RCL 6	25- 45 6
R↓	04- 33	X><Y	26- 34
STO 6	05- 44 6	−	27- 30
RCL 1	06- 45 1	R/S	28- 31
−	07- 30	RCL 8	29- 45 8
STO 7	08- 44 7	RCL 3	30- 45 3
RCL 5	09- 45 5	÷	31- 10
÷	10- 10	RCL 4	32- 45 4
R/S	11- 31	X	33- 20
RCL 7	12- 45 7	RCL 1	34- 45 1
RCL 4	13- 45 4	+	35- 40
÷	14- 10	R/S	36- 31
R/S	15- 31	RCL 6	37- 45 6
RCL 2	16- 45 2	X><Y	38- 34
RCL 1	17- 45 1	−	39- 30
−	18- 30	g GTO 00	40- 43, 33 00
STO 8	19- 44 8	f P/R	
RCL 5	20- 45 5		

REGISTERS			
n: Unused	i: Unused	PV: Unused	PMT: Unused
FV: Unused	R_0: Unused	R_1: RFR	R_2: R_m
R_3: S_m	R_4: S_p	R_5: B_p	R_6: $\overline{R}_p$
R_7: $\overline{R}_p-$RFR	R_8: $\overline{R}_m-$RFR	R_9-$R_{.4}$: Unused	

The calculations may be made as follows:

1. Key in the program.
2. Press $\boxed{f}$ CLEAR $\boxed{\text{REG}}$.
3. Key in the risk-free rate, as a percentage, and press $\boxed{\text{STO}}$ 1.
4. Key in the market's rate of return, as a percentage, and press $\boxed{\text{STO}}$ 2.
5. Key in the market's standard deviation, as a percentage, and press $\boxed{\text{STO}}$ 3.
6. Key in the actual return, as a percentage, of the asset or portfolio to be evaluated and press $\boxed{\text{ENTER}}$.
7. Key in the beta coefficient of the asset or portfolio and press $\boxed{\text{ENTER}}$.
8. Key in the standard deviation, as a percentage, of the asset or portfolio.
9. Press $\boxed{\text{R/S}}$ to calculate the Treynor ratio.
10. Press $\boxed{\text{R/S}}$ to calculate the Sharpe ratio.
11. Press $\boxed{\text{R/S}}$ to calculate the return predicted by using the security market line.
12. Press $\boxed{\text{R/S}}$ to calculate Jensen's alpha return on the basis of the return predicted by the security market line.
13. Press $\boxed{\text{R/S}}$ to calculate the return predicted by using the capital market line.
14. Press $\boxed{\text{R/S}}$ to calculate the alpha return on the basis of the return predicted by the capital market line.
15. For a new case, return to

a. Step 6 if the risk-free rate and the market's return and standard deviation are constant

b. Step 3 if these parameters change

Example 1:   Evaluate the performance of the following portfolios:

PORTFOLIO	AVERAGE REALIZED RETURN, PERCENT*	BETA	STANDARD DEVIATION, PERCENT
A	15.31	1.12	18.69
B	18.24	1.32	32.06
C	9.86	0.79	13.12
M†	13.97	1.00	19.24

*An analysis such as this one frequently uses annualized portfolio returns of quarterly or monthly returns over a past 5- to 10-year period.

†The market portfolio. The Standard & Poor's 500 Stock Index is frequently used as a proxy.

Note: Risk-free rate, 6.12%. The Treasury Bill rate is frequently used.

Keystrokes	Display	Comment
⨍ CLEAR REG	0.00	Clears registers.
6.12 STO 1	6.12	Stores the risk-free rate.
13.97 STO 2	13.97	Stores the market's average realized return.
19.24 STO 3	19.24	Stores the market's standard deviation.
		Portfolio A:
15.31 ENTER	15.31	Enters average realized return.
1.12 ENTER	1.12	Enters beta.
18.69	18.69	Enters standard deviation.
R/S	8.21	Treynor ratio.
R/S	0.49	Sharpe ratio.
R/S	14.91	SML predicted return.
R/S	0.40	Jensen's alpha return.
R/S	13.75	CML predicted return.
R/S	1.56	CML alpha return.
		Portfolio B:
18.24 ENTER	18.24	Enters average realized return.
1.32 ENTER	1.32	Enters beta.
32.06	32.06	Enters standard deviation.
R/S	9.18	Treynor ratio.
R/S	0.38	Sharpe ratio.
R/S	16.48	SML predicted return.
R/S	1.76	Jensen's alpha return.
R/S	19.20	CML predicted return.
R/S	−0.96	CML alpha return.
		Portfolio C:
9.86 ENTER	9.86	Enters average realized return.
.79 ENTER	0.79	Enters beta.
13.12	13.12	Enters standard deviation.
R/S	4.73	Treynor ratio.
R/S	0.29	Sharpe ratio.
R/S	12.32	SML predicted return.

Keystrokes	Display	Comment
R/S	−2.46	Jensen's alpha return.
R/S	11.47	CML predicted return.
R/S	−1.61	CML alpha return.

Jensen's alpha coefficient can also be estimated by regressing the portfolio's excess return or risk premium, $E(R_p)-RFR$, against the market's excess return premium, $E(R_m)-RFR$.

Example 2: The performance of a mutual fund and the market during the past 5 years has been as follows:

YEAR	MARKET	MUTUAL FUND	RISK-FREE RATE
1	0.115	0.142	0.042
2	−0.058	−0.079	0.051
3	−0.156	−0.122	0.059
4	0.184	0.213	0.043
5	0.232	0.327	0.040

Evaluate the performance of the mutual fund using the Jensen alpha measure.

Key in the HP-12C "beta coefficient" program that appears in Chapter 1, Section 1-2.

Keystrokes	Display	Comment
f CLEAR REG	0.00	Clears registers.
.142 ENTER .042 −	0.10	Risk premium returns, year 1.
.115 ENTER .042 −	0.07	
R/S	1.00	
.079 CHS ENTER .051 −	−0.13	Risk premium returns, year 2.
.058 CHS ENTER .051 −	−0.11	
R/S	2.00	
.122 CHS ENTER .059 −	−0.18	Risk premium returns, year 3.
.156 CHS ENTER .059 −	−0.22	
R/S	3.00	
.213 ENTER .043 −	0.17	Risk premium returns, year 4.
.184 ENTER .043 −	0.14	
R/S	4.00	
.327 ENTER .040 −	0.29	Risk premium returns, year 5.
.232 ENTER .040 −	0.19	
R/S	5.00	Total number of entries.
g GTO 03 R/S	0.03	Covariance.
R/S	0.15	Standard deviation of market's return.
R/S	0.18	Standard deviation of mutual fund's returns.
R/S	1.14	Beta coefficient.
R/S	0.03	Jensen alpha coefficient.

REFERENCES

1. Charles A. D'Ambrosio, *Principles of Modern Investments* (Science Research Associates, Chicago, 1976), chap. 20.
2. Frank K. Reilly, *Investment Analysis and Portfolio Management,* 2d ed., (Dryden Press, Hinsdale, Ill., 1985), chap. 22 and 26.

Chapter
SEVEN

OTHER INVESTMENT APPLICATIONS

Section
7-1
COMPOUND RATES
OF RETURN

Rates of return and rates of interest may be expressed as effective rates or as nominal rates. Since effective rates are compound rates, substantial differences in rates may occur depending on whether the return on an asset is compounded and, if so, how often during a year.

It is sometimes necessary to convert semiannual, quarterly, or monthly rates of return to annual compound rates of return, or vice versa.

The HP-12C "Owner's Handbook and Problem-Solving Guide" contains three programs designed to translate nominal rates to effective rates (pages 179–180), effective rates to nominal rates (pages 180–181), and nominal rates to continuous effective rates (page 181).

Example 1: During the first quarter of 1986, you obtained on your investments a total return of 5.3 percent. If this rate were compounded over the next three quarters, what would be your annual rate of return?*

---

*Use the procedure described on page 179 of the HP-12C "Owner's Handbook and Problem-Solving Guide."

Keystrokes	Display	Comment
f CLEAR FIN		
5.3 ENTER 4 × ENTER	21.20	Annual nominal rate.
4 n	4.00	Compounding periods.
÷ i	5.30	Quarterly rate of return.
100 CHS ENTER PV	−100.00	
FV +	22.95	Annual compound rate.

To determine the rate of return that must be earned every compounding period—e.g., month, quarter—in order to obtain a given annual rate of return,

1. Key in the desired annual rate of return and press ENTER.
2. Key in 1 and press +.
3. Key in the number of compounding periods and press 1/X Yˣ.
4. Key in 1 and press −.

Example 2:   You expect the S&P 500 Stock Index return to be 13 percent next year. What effective rate of return must you earn on your investments every month to obtain the same return as the S&P 500?

Keystrokes	Display	Comment
.13 ENTER	0.13	Enters annual rate of return.
1 +	1.13	
12 1/X Yˣ	1.01	
1 −	0.01	
f 4	0.0102	Monthly required rate of return.

To calculate the annual rate of return equivalent to a given rate of return earned every compounding period,

1. Key in the rate earned every compounding period and press ENTER .
2. Key in 1 and press +.
3. Key in the number of compounding period and press y^x.
4. Key in 1 and press −.

Example 3:   What will be your annual rate of return if you earn 3.75 percent each quarter?

Keystrokes	Display	Comment
.0375 ENTER	0.04	Enters quarterly rate of return.
1 +	1.04	
4 y^x	1.16	
1 −	0.16	
f 4	0.1587	Annual rate of return.

Section
7-2
TRANSACTION COSTS

Transaction costs have a significant effect on the rates of return that are earned or are expected to be earned by investors.

In the examples presented in this handbook, transaction costs have not been explicitly stated. When the purchase price of a security is referred to, the price paid by the investor should include the appropriate transaction costs. Similarly, when a security is sold at a given price, the appropriate costs should be deducted. By not explicitly including such transaction costs, we focused on the basic methods used to solve different problems with the HP-12C.

In calculating returns, transaction costs are easily considered by adding them to the purchase price to arrive at the cost price and subtracting them from the sale price to arrive at sale proceeds.

Once you master the use of the HP-12C, incorporating such costs in your calculations is easy.

REFERENCES

Bauman, W. Scott: *Estimating the Present Value of Common Stocks by the Variable Rate Methods* (Bureau of Business Research, Graduate School of Business Administration, University of Michigan, Ann Arbor, 1963).

Bookstaber, Richard M.: *Option Pricing and Strategies in Investing* (Addison-Wesley, Reading, Mass., 1981).

Cissell, R., H. Cissell, and D. C. Flaspohler: *Mathematics of Finance*, 6th ed. (Houghton Mifflin, Boston, 1982).

Cohen, Jerome B., Edward D. Zinbarg, and A. Zeikel: *Investment Analysis and Portfolio Management*, 4th ed. (Richard D. Irwin, Homewood, Ill., 1982).

D'Ambrosio, Charles A.: *Principles of Modern Investments* (Science Research Associates, Chicago, 1976).

Darst, David M.: *The Complete Bond Book: A Guide to All Types of Fixed-Income Securities* (McGraw-Hill Book Company, New York, 1975).

Elton, E. J., and M. J. Gruber: *Modern Portfolio Theory and Investment Analysis*, 2d ed. (John Wiley & Sons, New York, 1984).

Fischer, Donald E., and Ronald J. Jordan: *Security Analysis and Portfolio Management*, 3d ed. (Prentice-Hall, Englewood Cliffs, N.J., 1983).

Francis, Jack C.: *Investments: Analysis and Management*, 4th ed. (McGraw-Hill Book Company, New York, 1986).

Gitman, L. J., and M. D. Joehnk: *Fundamentals of Investing*, 2d ed. (Harper & Row Publishers, New York, 1984).

Graham, B., D. L. Dodd, S. Cottle, and Charles Tatham: *Security Analysis*, 4th ed. (McGraw-Hill Book Company, New York, 1962).

Greynolds, Elbert B., Julius S. Aronofsky, and Robert J. Frame: *Financial Analysis Using Calculators: Time Value of Money* (McGraw-Hill Book Company, New York, 1980).

Homer, Sidney, and Martin L. Leibowitz: *Inside the Yield Book: New Tools for Bond Market Strategy* (Prentice-Hall, Englewood Cliffs, N.J., 1972).

Huang, Stanley S. C.: *Investment Analysis and Management* (Winthrop Publishers, Cambridge, Mass., 1981).

Jenkins, James W.: *Self-Correcting Problems in Investment Management* (Allyn & Bacon, Boston, 1974).

Levine, Sumner N. (ed.): *Financial Analyst's Handbook I: Methods Theory and Portfolio Management* (Dow Jones–Irwin, Homewood, Ill., 1975).

————: *Financial Analyst's Handbook II: Analysis of Industry* (Dow Jones–Irwin, Homewood, Ill., 1975).

Reilly, Frank K.: *Investment Analysis and Portfolio Management*, 2d ed. (Dryden Press, Hinsdale, Ill., 1985).

Sharpe, William F.: *Investments*, 3d ed. (Prentice-Hall, Englewood Cliffs, N.J., 1985).

Smith, Keith V., and D. K. Eiteman: *Essentials of Investing* (Richard D. Irwin, Homewood, Ill., 1974).

Tinic, Seha M., and R. R. West: *Investing in Securities: An Efficient Market Approach* (Addison-Wesley Publishing Company, Reading, Mass., 1979).

Valentine, Jerome L., and E. A. Mennis: *Quantitative Techniques for Financial Analysis* (Richard D. Irwin, Homewood, Ill. 1980).

Appendix
FORMULAS

COMMON STOCKS (CHAPTER 1)

HOLDING-PERIOD RATE OF RETURN

R = single-period rate of return
$\overline{R}$ = arithmetic mean rate of return
G = geometric mean rate of return
P_1 = ending price
P_0 = beginning price
D_1 = dividend paid during designated period
n = number of observations
π = product of

SINGLE-PERIOD RATE OF RETURN

$$R = \frac{P_1 - P_0 + D_1}{P_0}$$

ARITHMETIC MEAN RATE OF RETURN

$$\overline{R} = \frac{\sum\limits_1^n R}{n}$$

GEOMETRIC MEAN RATE OF RETURN

$$G = [\pi(1+R)]^{1/n} - 1$$

COMMON STOCK RISK MEASUREMENTS

R_i = rate of return of dependent variable
R_m = rate of return of independent variable (normally, the market index)
$\overline{R}_i$ = arithmetic mean rate of return of dependent variable
$\overline{R}_m$ = arithmetic mean rate of return of independent variable
n = number of observations

STANDARD DEVIATION

$$S = \sqrt{\frac{\sum\limits_1^n (R - \overline{R})^2}{n}}$$

COEFFICIENT OF VARIATION
$$CV = \frac{S}{R}$$

COVARIANCE
$$COV_{im} = \frac{\sum\limits_{i=m=1}^{n} (R_i - \overline{R}_i)(R_m - \overline{R}_m)}{n}$$

BETA
$$B = \frac{COV_{im}}{S_m^2}$$

ALPHA
$$A = \overline{R}_m - b\,\overline{R}_i$$

COEFFICIENT OF CORRELATION
$$R_{im} = \frac{COV_{im}}{(S_i)(S_m)}$$

COEFFICIENT OF DETERMINATION
$$R_{im}^2 = \left[\frac{COV_{im}}{(S_i)(S_m)}\right]^2$$

STANDARD ERROR OF THE ESTIMATE
$$S_{im} = \sqrt{\frac{\sum\limits_{i=1}^{n} R_i^2 - A\sum\limits_{i=1}^{n} R_i - B\sum\limits_{i=m=1}^{n} R_i \times R_m}{n-2}}$$

HOLT'S GROWTH DURATION MODEL

P_g = current market price of a growth stock
P_a = current market price of a nongrowth stock
E_g = expected earnings per share of a growth stock
E_a = expected earnings per share of a nongrowth stock
$G(E_g)$ = average growth rate of earnings per share of a growth stock
$G(E_a)$ = average growth rate of earnings per share of a nongrowth stock
D_g = dividend yield of a growth stock
D_a = dividend yield of a nongrowth stock
L_n = base 10 logarithm
T = implied earnings growth rate duration

$$T = \frac{L_n\,[(P_g/E_g)/(P_a/E_a)]}{L_n\,[1 + G(E_g) + D_g/1 + G(E_a) + D_a)]}$$

BONDS (CHAPTER 2)

DURATION

C_t = annual coupon payments
P = par or redemption value
Y = yield to maturity on the bond
n = number of years left to maturity
D = duration

$$D = \frac{\displaystyle\sum_{t=1}^{2n} \frac{(C_{t/2})^t}{(1 + Y/2)^t} + \frac{(P)\,2n}{(1 + Y/2)^{2n}}}{\displaystyle\sum_{t=1}^{2n} \frac{C_{t/2}}{(1 + Y/2)^t} + \frac{P}{(1 + Y/2)^{2n}}}$$

WARRANTS AND CONVERTIBLE SECURITIES

CONVERTIBLE SECURITIES

CR = conversion ratio
CPP = conversion parity price
$CBPP$ = convertible bond purchase price
IV = investment value
n = years to maturity
C'_t = coupon of bonds equivalent to the convertible bond in maturity and quality but with no conversion features
r = investor's required rate of return
PV = par value
CV = conversion value
CSP = current stock price
$POIV$ = premium over investment value
$POCV$ = premium over conversion value
$CBMP$ = convertible bond market price
$TVCB$ = theoretical value convertible bond
N = years to conversion date
C_t = coupon of convertible bond
g = annual growth of stock price

CONVERSION PARITY PRICE

$$CPP = \frac{CBPP}{CR}$$

INVESTMENT VALUE	$IV = \sum_{t=1}^{2n} \dfrac{C'_{t/2}}{(1 + r/2)^t} + \dfrac{PV}{(1 + r/2)^{2n}}$
CONVERSION VALUE	$CV = CR \times CSP$
PREMIUM OVER INVESTMENT VALUE	$POIV = \left(\dfrac{CBMP - IV}{IV} \right) 100$
PREMIUM OVER CONVERSION VALUE	$POCV = \dfrac{CBMP - CV}{CV} \times 100$
THEORETICAL VALUE CONVERTIBLE BOND	$\mathrm{TVCB} = \sum_{t=1}^{2n} \dfrac{C_{t/2}}{(1 + r/2)^t} \dfrac{CSP(1+g)^N \times CR}{(1 + r/2)^t}$

INDEX

ABOUT THE AUTHORS

W. Scott Bauman, M.B.A., Ph.D., is a professor of finance and chairman of the Department of Finance, College of Business, Northern Illinois University. He is a Chartered Financial Analyst (CFA) and has served as Executive Director of The Institute of Chartered Financial Analysts.

Jaroslaw Komarynsky, M.B.A., Ph.D., is professor of finance at Northern Illinois University. He has been a security analyst in the trust department of the Continental Illinois National Bank & Trust Company of Chicago and has served as a member of the Education Committee of the Investment Analysts Society of Chicago.

John C. Siska Goytre, M.S., is an assistant representative in the Mexico City office of Continental Illinois National Bank & Trust Company of Chicago.